**Less Is The New More
Mindset Change For More Focus and Stress-free
Time Management**

Copyright © 2019 Chris Lee

chrisleespeaker.com

All rights reserved. This book or parts thereof may not be reproduced in any form, stored in any retrieval system, or transmitted in any form by any means—electronic, mechanical, photocopy, recording, or otherwise—without the prior written permission of the publisher, except as provided by United States of America copyright law. For permissions contact:

pr@chrisleespeaker.com

Cover by Jade.

Contents

- Intro 1
  - The Less Is More Mindset 6
- LESS Multitasking 8
  - Can you multitask? 9
  - But should you multitask? 12
  - The Stress Werewolf 17
  - 80/20 19
  - Your Core Art 24
  - Resist Shallow, Go A Little Deeper 28
  - 21 Day Mastery 32
  - Focus On Your My One 36
  - Mental Interrupts 42
  - Seriously, Just Focus 46
  - What Would Easy Look Like? 49
  - Your Core Time 52
  - Affirmation 57
  - LESS Multitasking Actions 60
- LESS Distractions 61
  - Why Do I Care? 62
  - Important Versus Urgent 65
  - Take Back Ownership Of Your Time 70
  - Email: The Great Distractor 72
  - Minimize the One-Offs 76
  - A Typical Work Day 80
  - Defer Social Media 83
  - The Art Of the Graceful "No" 88

- LESS Distractions Actions ... 93
- LESS Barriers ... 94
  - Less Friction ... 95
  - The Hemingway Method ... 97
  - Accountability Is Key ... 99
  - Coach For Accountability? ... 104
  - The 5 Second Rule ... 109
  - Start With The Acorn ... 113
  - Be A Time Squirrel ... 115
  - 168 Hours ... 117
  - Go Analog ... 122
  - The 3 Column Sticky System ... 125
  - The Minimum Viable Product ... 131
  - Manage Energy, Not Time ... 133
  - LESS Barriers Actions ... 138
- MORE Done ... 139
  - The Enjoy-Matters Matrix ... 140
  - Get 1% Better Every Day ... 147
  - Stop Lifting The Same Weights ... 149
  - Work-Life Balance ... 152
  - Having It All, Just Not At Once ... 154
  - Visualize Your Perfect Day ... 157
  - MORE Done Actions ... 160
  - Closing Words ... 161
- A request... ... 163
- Speaking Engagements ... 164

Intro

"The obscure we see eventually. The completely obvious, it seems, takes longer."
Edward R. Murrow

This quote by Edward R. Murrow[1] is something that always stuck with me over the years. We are complicated creatures, in a complex and colorful world, and so many times we get so distracted by the noise and pretty colors that we miss what is kind of obvious if we take a step back. In particular, what's completely clear to me now is we keep trying to *get more and more done*, but end up getting *less done*—of what really matters—because we get in our own way.

This book is the result of how I learned (eventually) to see and embrace what now seems completely obvious: I needed to slow down and *do less* in order to *get more done*. It seems counterintuitive, but in this book, I will convince you that it is not. And I wanted to share the above quote with you to assure you I am just as flawed and clueless sometimes as everyone else, but I was able to make a fundamental shift in my mindset, and you can too.

My mission for this book is to help people like you and me get control of their chaotic lives. People who have dreams and ambitions but find themselves working harder and harder and yet, never getting much closer to fulfilling those dreams. This is the best subject I could write about at this time, because it's about what helped me personally, and in doing so can help others like me. Also, it serves as a foundation for making improvements in other areas of our lives.

    I had a variety of topics I could have written about, and I found myself obsessing over picking the best direction to go, and how it would fit with my identify and brand, and if it was a buzzing topic, with a good keyword search. Because according to the experts you're supposed to think about *all* those things these days. But that just reminded me of when my life was getting crammed full with a growing list of things I needed to do or wanted to do, with the "needs" usually taking priority over my "wants" or passions. And it was causing me more and more stress and chaos as I tried to get it all done.

    Fortunately, at some point, I had an epiphany and eventually saw what now seems obvious: I needed to slow down and start doing less. That much was clear. But the problem was I still had a host of obligations as well as passions I didn't want to give up. I had studied a variety of productivity experts over the years—this was nothing new to me. But I usually felt like their recommendations were causing me more work with journal systems or complicated processes and it didn't resonate with me. But now, with my epiphany of slowing down and doing less, I could seek out and focus only on productivity ideas that would let me slow down but still get things done. By combining the advice of like-minded experts with my own experience and experiments, I developed the "Less Is More" mindset. To summarize:

    How can I slow down and do less, but still get the really important things done?

    It *seems* simple, but the opposite, which is the reality for many, many of us in today's multitasking, multichannel, always-on world is that we do MORE than we should and get LESS done, at least in terms of the things that really matter to us.

In doing so, I found "My One". I will talk about what that means later in the book, but in essence:

- My One is the *one thing* I can do *right now* that will make everything else better.
- That *one thing* is this Less Is More system, which I am going to share with you.

I'm not going to pretend I figured this all out by myself, because why would I? I want you to be encouraged by the fact that I have studied and tested a large variety of productivity experts and systems and cherry-picked the tactics that worked for me. Everyone and everything I discuss in this book is someone I believe in or something I have tested on myself.

And so, what I am going to do is share relevant principles and advice from other experts who I admire and whose ideas resonate with my own. Some of their ideas I put into practice and others I found resonated with my own concepts and experience.

I'm going to give you plenty of actionable advice-- enough to get your life and sanity back without needing to read anything else. But if you do want to take a deeper dive into any of these principles or methods, I whole-heartedly encourage it. And I stand by the quality of all the experts I talk about.

Let me also say that I don't want you to get the idea that I'm an easy-going type of person with simple wants and needs. And that I was born with the natural ability to just go with the flow and everything will be amazing. That is not who I am at all. People I work with have commented that they are amazed at how I can be so calm and patient sometimes. I absolutely assure you those have been acquired skills. I come from a long line of impatient, anxious people including my mother and her father, my grandfather. The apple (me) fell very close to the tree. I was the classic Type A, Fast Track person at work.

I am impatient by nature, and while I am a happy person, I am also perpetually unsatisfied to a degree and always want to accomplish more and squeeze a little more out of life.

I am telling you this to help you believe that:

- You aren't out of luck if you are not a laid back, carefree person by nature.
- You are not doomed if you are prone to multitasking and doing everything at once.
- You *can* have it all, or at least a lot of what's important, if you learn to approach it differently.
- You are not alone if you feel like life is piling up, and there has to be a better way.

The principles and tactics I'm going to teach you, I've had to learn through a lot of research, patience and trial and error. And it's a lifelong journey as society and technology come up with new ways to complicate our lives, and the media creates more ways for us to feel disappointed in ourselves. I hope to save you the time I spent figuring this out and help you fulfill your goals and desires but in a low-stress way.

I'm not going to ask you to settle for less. I'm going to help you achieve more with less effort, less stress, and more enjoyment of the journey.

Note that this time reboot strategy is a process, and several of us authors are supporting the movement with different perspectives and pieces of the puzzle. Our ideas do and should overlap in various ways. It's rare for any author to come up with radically new material and I claim no exception. My work comes from studying and building on the work of past and present authorities on time management. By adding my own experiences and perspective, I hope to help others transform their own lives.

While reflecting on the multiple research areas I'm involved in, reclamation of time and stress reduction stood out as critical for not only improving productivity, but also for *quality-of-life* across the board. I believe quality-of-life is a critical aspect of getting-things-done. Not addressing this aspect of your life is a sure recipe for burnout. To drive this point home, let me share a quote from Mark Manson:

"Every productivity book on the planet, from David Allen to Benjamin Franklin, tells you more or less the same thing: wake up at the ass-crack of dawn and drink some stimulating liquid, segment your work periods into bite-sized chunks organized by urgency and importance, keep fastidious lists and calendars, and schedule appointments 15 weeks in advance and be early to everything."[2]

I don't think I could do that for long. I certainly don't *want* to do that for long. With this book, I will show you what I do instead and still get more done.

The Less Is More system guides you through the principles and tactics of its first three pillars:

LESS Multitasking
LESS Distractions
LESS Barriers

Embracing and acting on these three pillars will set you free--free to find the productivity and success you are striving for and go on to achieve with the fourth pillar:

MORE Done!

Let's get started.

The Less Is More Mindset

Less Is More is about slowing down to feel better about what you accomplish. *Less Is More* is about tactics to focus on what matters. But above all else, *Less Is More* is a mindset. You must believe that you can slow down and still get stuff done. You must learn to internalize the feeling that's it's ok *not to do* certain things right away, and sometimes *not do them ever*. In short, you must have a mindset that *believes* this is possible.

I don't expect you to believe that right now. But I fully expect to get you to believe it, by revealing not only my own perspective and experience but also backing it with strategies and perspectives from other experts. I will also give you my best *actionable* tactics for getting more of the things done that really matter.

In the modern world—and certainly in America—it's all about massive consumption and *more is more*. More TV channels, bigger meal portions, more possessions, and more "friends." We're all about going big or going home. And reality TV has shown us there is no limit yet to how large, extreme or ridiculous we can be and still get attention or how far we can push the limits.

But when we push the limits too far, at least in all areas of our life and for too long, it will inevitably take a toll on our body, mind, and spirit.

You can find many examples where more, or at least too much, is not even satisfying, let alone good for you. When you get overloaded with too much of anything, even a good thing, it becomes more of a blur, and you aren't able to fully appreciate the nuances or give enough time to important moments.

It's like bodybuilding. Both women and men look better with good muscles and muscle tone. But in either case—men or women—too much muscle starts to look gross and become a turn-off instead of appealing.

There are exceptions where bigger may be better, for example in certain grown-up situations which I will leave to your imagination. But even in those situations, arguments can be made that just enough is better than too much.

Less Is More is not about minimalism, at least not exactly; it's about doing just enough and no more. It's about actually getting more done by doing less of what you've been doing, but doing the right things at the right time.

LESS Multitasking

Can you multitask?

One of the first issues we need to tackle is the subject of multitasking. It's a topic that's been in vogue among writers and bloggers lately--actually for some time--and they speak about the evils of multitasking when it comes to productivity and getting things done. A popular article even goes so far as to say humans *can't* multitask, and call it "The Myth Of Multitasking."[1]

As you will see shortly, I have some thoughts and counterarguments against this "fact." However, I *also agree* that multitasking is a big problem so I would like to spend a minute talking about it. First, the arguments against the idea that you can't multitask:

Number one: the human brain is the most highly advanced parallel processor on the planet. At least it is at the time of this writing. Maybe one day a supercomputer AI will win that title, but despite what science fiction movies show, we really aren't that close.

My graduate research was in the areas of neural networks and machine intelligence, so I feel I can make my case with some authority. You could argue at what level the brain can multitask, but it's sufficient to say that at some level, or at several levels, it can and does.

Argument number two: At the exact time I am writing this section I am sitting in a busy Starbucks with my laptop, sipping on a bold roast coffee, surrounded by people and noise and some (chill) music playing in my earbuds. And it's going pretty well. I am able to think and type and selectively process sounds in my hearing. I am confident of that last part because my brain has been tuning out all the usual Starbucks noise--until I heard a barista call out the name "Chris" for someone else's order (I already had mine, so I wasn't listening for it). Thank God, the universe, and my common name for having this happen at *just the right time* to make my point.

My final, and favorite, argument: I am a part-time singer-songwriter. To perform as a singer-songwriter requires me to:

- Play my guitar
- Sing
- Monitor and respond to the reaction of the crowd
- And sometimes other things (for example following a partner's pitch if singing a duet)

All these things have to happen at the same time. There is no opportunity for single-tasking, switch-tasking, or whatever you choose to call it. I am not saying it's easy—in fact it takes a lot of practice. And these are not low-level activities you can just learn at the reflex level such that they function like breathing or walking. No, they are higher level cognitive tasks that require conscious thought activity. So no-one will ever convince me that humans can't multitask. You don't have to be a singer-songwriter to appreciate what I'm saying. If you are reading this, chances are you are an experienced driver. You can legitimately argue that texting while driving is not so doable, but on the other hand "driving while driving" requires doing several mental tasks at the same time, or at least doing them in an efficient task-switching way.

And last but not least, it may be a little insulting to you.

If I tell you that multitasking isn't possible, and you're there multitasking like a boss—well, my credibility won't be too great, will it?

Sorry for my mini rant, but I felt obligated to address the argument, because too often I hear experts flippantly throw out "facts" which contradict what I experience personally, as well as what I gather from the field. I believe productivity advice and strategies should be based on sound facts and observations and not the hand-waving arguments that are in vogue at the moment. Any strategy not based on sound research has a shaky foundation and will probably not stand the test of time.

Now, in the next chapter, let's consider the arguments for *not multitasking*. Because the *need to focus* at appropriate times is actually *really crucial,* and you're going to hear me talk about it repeatedly in following chapters.

Addendum: The barista just called the order for yet another "Chris." I sure do have a popular name. As well as the ability to multitask.

But should you multitask?

"But *should* you multitask?"
Me, right now.

    This--is a totally different question. The short answer is "way less than you probably do now." At least for concentrated or "deep work." "Deep work" is another phrase that seems to be popular these days among productivity experts and probably means different things to different people. But for our purposes we'll just say deep work means a task requiring a significant amount of time and attention to detail, because it's your core art or is otherwise important and deserves your best effort. Your core art, which I will discuss more later, is basically whatever is your passion.
    In one way or another, most of the productivity experts I refer to in this book advise focusing on a few, or just one, important task. And of course, the central philosophy of this book--Less Is More--implies you will be doing less *in general* and so it makes sense to do less *at the same time*.
    On the other hand, it's nearly impossible to completely avoid multitasking in real life. Sometimes it's unavoidable because your manager, child or your own life requires attention in some manner that you can't ignore or put off until later. Using the mindset and principles in this book you can work on reducing or eliminating some of these distractions. But you can't not feed your children, or yourself, on a regular schedule. You could also choose to give up on personal hygiene, but I wouldn't recommend it (thanks--for all of us). And telling your boss you won't be

doing that urgent report right now is what we call a "career-limiting" decision.

The world is rarely black and white, and so it is with multi-tasking and single-tasking. As I discussed in the previous chapter, you can multi-task some things, and the result is you can get more work done in your available time to some degree--if you do it right and don't do it excessively. My recommendation, which I will repeat several times in this book, is that you do focused, single-tasking work, on your core art, in the morning, when your energy and mental sharpness is at its peak. And then use some of the rest of your available work time for multi-tasking the urgent-but-not-important, the "one-offs" (covered later), basic needs, etc.

You should also single-task the quality time you spend on your relationships, or relationship building. I am not going to lecture you on the evils of texting, web surfing or doing social media. These things are pretty amazing. But I will adamantly maintain they are not appropriate when you're spending relationship time with someone else whether it be a significant other, family, friends or your business tribe.

So your time will generally involve these three kinds of work:

1. Single-tasking, focused deep work on your core art. Find a way to do this on several or most of your mornings.
2. Multi-tasking other non-core-art work, urgent-but-not-important requests, and other productivity drainers like email and social media. I recommend doing this during the middle of the day when you are working your day job or otherwise tied to other people's schedules and needs.
3. In the evening (generally), plan quality single-tasking time for relationships. If you have more time to work on your art in the evening, or your

particular schedule requires it, then great, go ahead and do that. But don't do it so much that you neglect your relationships.

From a Less Is More mindset, this approach accomplishes your goal of focusing on your core art and reducing some of the time wasters such that your life is less hectic and stressful.   But it does so in a way that doesn't require unrealistic life changes (like telling your boss to shove it, or running away from your needy family).

Summary:
Single-task your core art and important relationships.
Multi-task the urgent and less important (for you) things.

The Stress Werewolf

A big part of the stress that comes with getting things done--and it certainly was for me--is getting frustrated when the day is progressing, and you feel like you're not getting done what you really wanted to do. The reason is that you are more emotionally connected with, and invested in, your core art, so when you don't get these tasks done, it affects your mental and emotional state much more than other tasks.

You may be getting all kinds of tasks done during the day, but they aren't what matter to you, so you have this nagging feeling in the back of your mind that slowly builds over the day leaving you stressed and frustrated that once again you didn't get done what you had hoped to do. So you roll over those important core art items on your to-do list to the next day, sleep, wake up and likely repeat the same pattern; failing again to get done what you wanted. So you experience this source of building stress, day after day, week after week--even year after year. It's no wonder you feel unfulfilled.

And others may tell you just to relax and let it go, but you and I aren't wired that way because we have goals, and dreams to chase, and art to get out of our heads and into the world to share with other people. So we compulsively read self-help books and study motivational courses in the hope of finding some way to get relief from this stress that didn't have a name (until now). Meanwhile this stress is always there, like a lurking stress werewolf breathing down your neck and threatening to eat away at your sanity.

I won't promise that Less Is More will solve all your problems. In fact I wouldn't listen to anyone who would make such a bold claim. I *will* tell you that adopting a Less Is More mindset can most definitely be the silver bullet you need to kill this stress werewolf preying on your sanity and well-being. By learning over time--using baby steps as necessary from the different chapters in this book--you *can* learn to focus more on your core art and what's important, and spend less time on what is not.

And specifically, when you learn to get your core art tasks done early in the day, you will start to feel the effect of this particular stress melting away. When you get even just the One core art task done in the morning or at least by the time your lunch period is over, then the stress dissipates instead of building up all day.

You can relax more, with a feeling of accomplishment and fulfillment that you got something of value done today. And then you can deal with those urgent-but-not-important things without feeling anxiety or resentment. If you get more core art or priority work done in the rest of the day, then great. But it's not required--it's icing on the cake. And in the evening, you won't be waiting until 10 pm to try and get some work done when you now are totally exhausted. Instead, you can relax in the evening and spend quality time with your relationships, doing fitness, reading and/or planning your tomorrow at a leisurely pace.

Summary:
Embrace the Less Is More Mindset and tactics to get core art done early, and defeat the Stress Werewolf.

How do you like my stress werewolf--silver bullet analogy?

80/20

"The 80/20 Principle--that 80 percent of results flow from just 20 percent of our efforts--is one of the great secrets of highly effective people and organizations."
Richard Koch

Ok, let's start talking about actual tactics and principles. One of the most relevant and time-tested principles for productivity is the "80/20 Principle" (also known as the "80/20 Rule" or "Pareto Principle") which was discovered by Italian economist Vilfredo Pareto in the 19th century and has been observed or validated many times and in many places since then. Some examples include:

- 80% of Italy's land was owned by 20% of the population (Pareto's original observation)
- 20% of the workers produce 80% of the results
- 20% of the customers create 80% of the revenue
- 20% of software bugs cause 80% of the crashes
- 20% of the product features result in 80% of the usage
- 20% of the earners have paid roughly 80% of Federal income taxes
- *20% of the effort produces 80% of the project*

Whether the numbers always work out exactly to 20 and 80 percent is not important because this pattern has played out over and over again in a variety of studies and projects. Repeatedly, the majority of the impact (good or bad) comes from the minority of whatever is being measured.

Richard Koch explored the 80/20 Principle extensively in his aptly titled book *The 80/20 Principle, The Secret Of Achieving More With Less.*[1] Koch summarized the principle like this:

> *"The 80/20 Principle—that 80 percent of results flow from just 20 percent of our efforts—is one of the great secrets of highly effective people and organizations."*

This is the aspect of 80/20 that we are most interested in for the purposes of this book. The good news is that 80% of your achievement and success will come from roughly 20% of your efforts. The bad news is that 80% of your effort will be wasted on unproductive activities. For maximum effectiveness we need to address both of these situations: we want to maximize the time we spend doing the productive 20% things and minimize the time we spend on the wasteful, counterproductive 80% activities.

You could spend some time doing a detailed analysis of how you spend your time and score how productive each activity is. You could certainly do that, and it might be worth it if you have the time.

However, I have an easier way for you:

Apply the 80/20 Principle to itself and just quickly identify and start focusing on your most productive activities--the "low hanging fruit."

In other words, just identify the few most important activities that come to your mind, and that is your 20%. Then stop there and don't overthink it, because everything else is your unproductive 80%. But still, how do you know your efforts are being targeted toward the right 20% goals? This is how:

* * *

Use your emotional reaction to identify the activities you are drawn to be doing.

Any activity that you aren't drawn to, or driven to, emotionally is one you don't want to be doing in the long run. Unless you are actually lazy--and I'm assuming you aren't if you are reading this--then if you don't really want to do something, it's something you need to stop doing, or at least do less of. I know that sounds too simple and you will probably immediately identify a bunch of things you have to do or else you will lose your job, or kids or spouse, etc. I understand. This is a guiding principle, not something you will do overnight or need to do completely.

Also, if you think about your tasks, you will probably agree with me that you find some unnecessary or even ridiculous. You're just stuck doing them at this point. So let's work on getting you unstuck. The following are two lists of categories to help you out. The first lists kinds of activities that are low value and the second lists things that are high value. Use these to help evaluate if your tasks are high or low value. They are general enough to apply across a wide variety of job roles.

Low Value Activities
- Things other people want you to do
- Things you do only because they've always been done this way
- Things you are not particularly good at (and not passionate about learning)
- Things you don't enjoy doing
- Things that always get interrupted
- Things where your partners are unreliable or low quality
- Things that have a predictable cycle
- Answering the telephone
- Things that distract you from your core art or

purpose
- Social media, TV, or any form of passive consumption
- Things you do only because someone made the most noise
- Things controlled by gatekeepers
- Things that require other's validation

High Value Activities
- Things that advance your overall purpose in life
- Things that you have always wanted to do
- Innovative ways to slash the time required and/or multiply the results
- Things other people say can't be done
- Things other people have done successfully in a different area
- Things that use your own creativity
- Things that you can get other people to do for you with relatively little effort on your part
- Anything with high-quality collaborators
- Things for which it is now or never
- Things your role models do that you admire
- Time with people who make you feel energized instead of drained
- Things for which you can actually measure significant results
- Things that truly help other people without being asked, or doing their job for them
- Things that let you make fast, easy decisions--no-brainers
- Things that have given you a positive impact in the past

Your goal is to do more high-value activities and minimize the low-value activities. I used the word "minimize" because I understand that there will be things you really have to do that you don't want to. So you can eliminate some tasks but others you want to find a way to minimize by, putting them off, delegating or doing the absolute minimum.

Breaking Out Of Your Comfort Zone

Before I leave this section, I want to touch on this important point: some activities you aren't doing because they cause you anxiety and require you to step out of your comfort zone. *These are almost always your highest value activities* and should be in your 20%. Again, use your emotional reaction to identify these. Your anxiety is not a bad emotion--it's the sign that achieving some goal will lead to an even more positive emotional state of accomplishment. Don't avoid these activities, embrace them. Other chapters in this book will help you get there.

Exercise: Use the above lists as a guide to make a simple two-column chart. In the first column, you list specific activities you do, or want to do, that are high value. In the second column list low-value activities you need to stop, minimize or avoid doing.

Summary:
The 80/20 Principle is simple math that will set you free.
Identify your most high value activities (the 20%) and focus on them. Minimize the other 80%.

Your Core Art

"The work you do while you procrastinate is probably the work you should be doing for the rest of your life."[1]
Jessica Hische

I don't know Jessica Hische, but she sounds like my kind of person. Procrastination gets a bad rap because often it is revealing a deeper truth that you should be spending your time doing something else. Remember when you were a child and much of your time was spent doing, or at least thinking about, exactly what interested you and what you were passionate about? How do we lose that? Yeah, ok, we grow up and have responsibilities, but the sad truth is over time we let the pendulum of work-life balance swing way over to the work side where it gets stuck.

A key concept to the Less Is More strategy is your "core art." Basically:

You need to spend as much of your time as you can focusing on your core art.

That simple statement is paramount to embracing Less Is More and getting more done of what matters. To drive that message home I am going to give you another quote from Derek Sivers, musician, founder of CDBaby, and expert on getting more of the important things done:

"Whatever excites you, go do it. Whatever

drains you, stop doing it."[2]
Derek Sivers

Sivers calls this your "compass" because you should use it as your guide. In his words "You have to pay close attention to that compass, even in little day-to-day decision ... If it doesn't excite you, don't do it. There's almost nothing that you must do."[3]

My version of Sivers' advice is that you must focus on your core art. But what do I mean, exactly, when I say your "core art"? Some experts and systems like to refer to your "core competency," and the principle is generally applied in the same way but I want to make an important distinction. Your "core competency" (or competencies) refers to what you are good at and what makes you valuable to *others*. Your "core art" means what you are passionate about and gives meaning and value to *yourself*.

If you are lucky, they are the same. Unfortunately often they are not. I am in this situation myself. I have always been good at technology such as computers and designing software. However I am most passionate about music: songwriting, playing guitar and singing.

I hear similar stories many, many times from other working professionals. Their core competency is what they do and what makes them a good living, but they secretly or publicly want to pursue a different passion or art.

And the reality is that most people have more than one passion. Some people have a single passion and are happy doing that for their entire life. But I believe many people have multiple passions they want to pursue in their lifetime. A business professional may be passionate about developing new technology, running a business, accounting, health care or similar traditional white collar professions. And they pursued that passion and became good at it and made a good living at it. But along the way, they had to give up other passions like music, painting, fitness challenges etc. And they are stuck doing their core competency, but their core art or passion now lies somewhere else.

Similarly a starving artist may be passionate about doing something that will let them grow business skills or give them more opportunity to travel or help others.

So I will talk about "core art" as the thing, the current passion, that is driving you to grow yourself, expand your horizons or make you feel more self-fulfilled. And as such, it is the thing that if you spent more time doing it would make you happier. It does not have to be something artistic in the classic sense such as music, painting or dance (but it certainly may be). Maybe you are passionate about learning computer programming or accounting or becoming a talented pastry chef. I consider those--and anything else you want to learn to be great at--your art.

How do you find your core art? It's not that hard--it's what you are passionate about and drawn to. Well, there may be a hard part: being clear on what you are really, persistently passionate about versus what is your passion trend of the moment. To help answer this question, ask yourself these questions?

- What do you spend your free time doing?
- What do you spend your non-free time doing?

And more importantly: what passion has persisted over time? What did you want to do when you were 8 years old? Or 18 years old? Is there something from back then you are still passionate about? Something that makes your mood light up whenever you hear about it or think about it? That thing that just won't go away?

Whenever I hear someone casually throw out a motivational quote along the lines of "If you love what you do you'll never work a day in your life" it makes me think they're delusional or not being quite honest. Every job involves a lot of hard work and tasks you begrudge doing whether it's administrative work, selling yourself or business or invoicing (i.e., getting paid).

Still, if it's your true passion you will want to do it year after year and can't imagine doing something else--despite the mundane tasks and hard work that goes along with it.

I could go on and on about this philosophically, but for our purposes, philosophy is not much help without some real, tactical advice to make it work. And that's exactly what I'll be sharing, so let's continue.

Summary:
Spend as much of your time as you can focusing on your core art

Whatever excites you, do it. Whatever drains you, stop doing it.

Resist Shallow, Go A Little Deeper

Whether you've already heard about the evils of multitasking, or are just hearing now from me, saying it is one thing and actually making the necessary changes in practice turns out to be a whole other matter, even when we "get it." Why is that?

The basic reason is we have many opposing forces demanding our attention. Or to be accurate, I should say we have new forces demanding our attention like the Internet, our smartphones and TV (if you want to call that new). Our ancestors had to pay attention to a lot of things too which we don't worry about so much--like listening for animals that could eat them. The fundamental difference is our ancestors' attention was focused on the real sensory world immediately around them whereas our attention is being diverted to virtual areas in the cloud and away from the people and environment in front of us.

We make excuses and say, it's the new way of the world. And we talk about how Millennials are learning how to multitask better and process multiple inputs at once. Sure, a lot of Millennials--and let's be honest: many non-Millennials--may have learned to watch and skim multiple channels of media. But at what cost? What are the trade-offs?

I majored in and studied intelligence and cognitive thinking, so I can fairly confidently assure you that the fundamental architecture of the human brain did not change in one generation. As one proof, after thousands of years, we still have the same sleep mechanisms and requirements, and over and over again we see the peril when we ignore it. While the human mind is amazingly plastic and adaptable and varies to some degree across individuals and genders, the architecture is the same--only the contents vary. So I refute the claim that Millennials are significantly better at multitasking than anyone else, and I will also argue against any claim that they've lost the ability for deep attention.

At most we've prioritized and honed some skills and capabilities compared to others, in the same way athletes, scholars and artists hone respectively different skills. But athletes can learn arts, and artists can learn to program. So my point is none of us are much different in terms of our brain's capabilities.

I also argue against the idea that shallow attention and interactions are the way of the future. Here are some ways we've suffered:

- People's eyes glued to their smartphones while ignoring the people sitting right in front of them. This is happening more in a variety of situations including home life, social settings, and even business situations.
- Even outside of smartphones, the nature of social interactions has been changing in bad ways, becoming more shallow and resulting in things like causal hookups. I can best summarize this with a real quote I heard recently from an attractive, intelligent, personable woman who was re-entering the dating world "Dating has changed, and I hate it."
- In business meetings I frequently see people bringing their laptops and using them to do other tasks and answer email--basically anything other than participating in the topic at hand. I started making a conscious effort to leave my laptop at my desk while attending meetings.
- As parents, we tend to use TV, games and the Internet as babysitters. I have been just as guilty and believe me I appreciate the bliss of being able to

occupy a child for a while by handing them a device or putting on a movie or TV show and getting a stress break. But when we rely on it too much as a crutch, the relationship suffers. More to the point: I've noticed even movie night dynamics have changed. Instead of gathering to lounge and share some popcorn and make witty or snarky comments about the movie, we tend to multitask with other devices, and people even wander off mid-movie to do something else.

What's happening is we are honing some new skills and practices that aren't necessarily bad, but are negatively impacting our social interactions and also productivity. What matters is how, when, and how often you choose to use them. The whole point of most self-help books and programs is to teach us how to most effectively use our potential.

This sometimes means unlearning bad habits. How do we do this? Other sections in this book will provide a mindset and tactics which give you more control over your focus and help avoid the negative habits. But there are some specific tactics we can also use:

- Practice being mindful about focusing your attention on one thing. This could be a person, computer, smartphone or nature. All have their time and place but focus on one at a time.
- If you're with a person, especially on a date or social situation, just put the phone away. Period. Make eye contact--it's a thing.
- If you're in a business meeting, focus on the presenter foremost, and also the presenters. If you need to take notes, be very careful only to do that. For many meetings now, whether with a group or a face-to-face, I don't take notes on my laptop or even on pad and paper. This usually allows me to

internalize all the important details anyway.
- If you're watching a movie, focus on the movie and enjoy its nuances as well as your mutual enjoyment with your companion(s).
- And finally, make your interactions work for you. It's surprising what you can learn from many otherwise boring situations. If you don't like the conversation steer it in a more interesting and positive direction. See what you can learn. It's usually a win-win situation.

Summary:
Resist shallow interactions, focus and go a little deeper.

21 Day Mastery

"There's just one rule: NO phone, NO email, and NO interruptions. None. When you do that for 3 weeks, you'll have mastery over a block of time and have the confidence and training for more."
Ed Rush

For some time it has been asserted that it takes 21 days to form a new (hopefully good) habit or break a bad habit. As with many other things, experts are debating if it's really 21 days, or 66 days, or something else. Since I don't care to wait while the "experts" figure this out, I'll continue to use 21 days as a rough guide, and I believe it's a reasonable target and working timeline for learning a new skill or a new task.

Part of the reason the 21-day strategy works is because it uses the more general principle called "time-boxing." Time-boxing means you set a fixed time period during which a particular project, task or chunk of work *must be accomplished*. In other words, you set the goal for what must be finished at the end of the time-box (for example 21 days) and then do everything in your power the make that deadline. It's a very effective strategy because it forces you to stop procrastinating and to make quick decisions instead of spinning your wheels.

Ed Rush is a good poster child for the 21-day timeline. Rush is a decorated F-18 fighter pilot, whose career included over 50 combat missions and 2 tours in Iraq. He later drew upon his military career and experience to become a motivational speaker and writer, authoring the book: *The 21 Day Miracle: How To Change Anything in 3*

Short Weeks.¹ Rush delivers his message in an entertaining and often hilarious style. As an example, he claims to have achieved all of this "despite possessing a below average intelligence." And even failing Kindergarten.² Even if that's not true, it's funny--I don't care who you are.

But make no mistake, Rush is serious about getting things done and believe many miraculous changes are possible in just 21 days. He further gives several specific templates for how to accomplish a particular change or "mastery" in 21 days. Examples include "The 21-Day Mind Mastery Miracle", "The 21-Day Money Mastery Miracle", and "The 21-Day Time Freedom Miracle" (a personal favorite). At the time of this writing you could still sign up at his website and get the templates for free.³

Here is a summary of his approach for accomplishing great things with the 21-day timeframe:

Start Small. Grow Big.

One of the biggest reasons people fail at "time management" is because they take on too much at once. Then they end up quitting because it becomes too hard.

So instead, manage your time starting in 30 minute blocks. As you learn to discipline your time and your mindset for short periods, you can then expand them to larger periods of 1, 2 or 4 hours.

Consistent with the-21 day approach, take exactly 30-minutes a day to do one uninterrupted activity. To quote Rush: "There's just one rule: NO phone, NO email, and NO interruptions. None. When you do that for three weeks, you'll have mastery over a block of time and have the confidence and training for more."

Fire Your Time Leeches

As I will also cover in more detail in the *LESS*

Distractions section, a regrettable but necessary pillar to getting anything done is managing people who will drain your time away like "Time Leeches."

Managing the time leeches usually means avoiding them for long periods. Trying to reason with them usually doesn't work, because you will not be able to change their belief that their time is more important than yours.

Tactics for avoiding interruptions from these people include:

- Closing your door. That means literally, physically closing your door if you work in an office environment. Not closing the door on them metaphorically, though you can do that too.
- Turn off your phone or put it into airplane mode.
- Get off of email while you are doing your focused work. (More on that in a later section)
- Tell everyone who works for you or with you, "I'm going to be busy for the next 3 hours. Only interrupt me for an emergency. An emergency is defined as 'life-threatening' or 'Someone is bleeding' or 'Your wife went into labor,' and not defined as 'I'm late on this report, so do you have time to look at my spreadsheet?'"

Turn Off Notifications

This is worth repeating these days: go to the settings on your phone and turn ALL notifications off. Seriously, turn them all off. No icons, sounds, or notification badges. You need to block all the interruptions from Facebook, Instagram, text messages, and the hundred other things on your phone that want to notify you. If you really have a notification addiction and need help with this you can actually get an app to help you with this, as I discuss in my later chapter "Defer Social Media."

To employ a 21-day strategy, you can go to Rush's

website as referenced above. Or you can use this simple strategy:

- Find a blank calendar (one without dates), which you can do by Googling for it. You could print out the current month, but this could be a problem if you start halfway in a month.
- Print out the calendar sheet and fill in the dates for the 21 sequential days (if you use an unnumbered calendar).
- Declare your goal to be accomplished by the end of the 21 days. Write this at the top of the sheet.
- Hang this sheet on your wall in a highly visible place.
- Every day, do some work toward the goal and then physical cross off the date on the sheet with an 'X.' Use a red marker to make the 'X' if possible.

It might seem silly to you, but it's important to follow the above steps as closely as you can. In other words, you must hang a physical paper sheet on the wall and cross off dates as you go. It has been proven over and over again that this is more effective because it has a stronger psychological effect for self-motivating you. Once you get started, you'll find you hate the thought of missing a day and not making that red 'X.'

As far as doing the actual work, you can and should use other tactics from this book to help keep you focused and on track. For example, you can use the "3 Column Sticky System" I describe later to break down the mastery goal into subtasks and start knocking them off during the 21 days.

Summary:
Use the 21 Day time-boxing approach to start "mastering" goals.

Focus On Your My One

"What's the ONE Thing you can do such that by doing it everything else will be easier or unnecessary?"
Gary Keller

If you want your Less Is More mindset to really work for you, you're going to want to learn how to *focus on one project at a time*, which I call "My One." Specifically your My One is the current most important project related to your core art. If it's not your core art or not directly furthering it, then it is not your My One. Further, it is not "My Two" or "My Three" even if it's related to your core art —it is one and only one project you work on until completion.

To help clarify, your My One is a milestone task or project that can be completed in a reasonable timeframe— let's use anywhere from a week to 90 days as a guideline. It is an important achievement that furthers your long-term career or artistic goal, but not the end goal itself. It's also generally not a quick task you can do in an hour or less. You will, however, break it down into such tasks which you will focus on completing on a daily basis. In summary the best My One is something that's not so long that you can't see progress and get demotivated and not so short that it's a trivial accomplishment.

Gary Keller is an author who has built a complete philosophy around the One concept. Keller calls it "The ONE Thing," which he discusses in his aptly titled book: *The ONE Thing: The Surprisingly Simple Truth Behind Extraordinary Results*.[1]

Like myself and others, Keller was highly influenced by Pareto's 80/20 Principle. But in Keller's words: "He doesn't go far enough." Keller wants you to take Pareto to the extreme, to go even smaller by identifying the vital few of the few, until you arrive at the vital "one." This is your essential "ONE Thing."

In different words, Keller's book and philosophy are based around a simple but powerful question, one he calls the "Focusing Question":

"What's the ONE Thing you can do such that by doing it everything else will be easier or unnecessary?"

What is the *one* thing?--not a few things, not the top things plural.

Side Note: What Keller calls "The ONE Thing" I like to call your "My One." Tricky grammar aside, I prefer this because I want you to internalize "My One" and use it as a guiding principle to ask yourself: "What is My One?" "Am I working on My One?" You can even use it in an affirmation:
"I am focusing on My One..."

By the way, if you're wondering if Keller or his system is legit or effective, consider that he is the founder of "Keller Williams," which is one of the largest, if not largest, real estate companies in the world. I know I can safely say he has my attention.

The focusing question is deceptively simple for a couple of reasons. One reason is because it can be used at multiple levels. It helps you answer the big picture questions like:

- What is my core art?
- What is the one thing I can contribute to the world?
- When I look back at my life, what is the one I can't have missed?

- Basically, who do I want to be when I grow up?

But the Focusing Question also helps answer all the small and medium questions along the path to getting to the big picture:

- What is the ONE thing I should do with my life? This is your "someday" goal.
- What ONE thing should be my current project to move toward my someday goal?
- What is the ONE thing I should do right now to achieve my current project?

The other reason the Focusing Question is deceptively simple is that it is deceptively *hard.* You're going to have to make choices, some of them being the hard choices. It's very difficult to pick one of anything in life, especially if you are a multitasker by nature or necessity. It relatively easy to name off the few things that are your top priorities or passions but it can be incredibly hard to pick just one. It's like asking you to pick your favorite child.

The Domino Effect

Keller relates the process and success of The ONE Thing to what he calls the "Domino Effect." On its own, a domino isn't much. Further, even a bunch of dominos that have no organization will accomplish little to nothing.

But—each domino has the capability of knocking down another one that is 1.5x its size. Properly lined up one after another, the progression of dominos can produce an amazing outcome.

The key to success, then, is figuring out your one most important thing in your career or life over the long-run—your "someday" goal. Once you've figured that out, you need to identify all the right dominoes you need to line up--and then knock down--in order to achieve it.

The ONE Thing philosophy is very much in line with the

Less Is More philosophy because it is continuously identifying the right "dominoes" to line up, which is the same as identifying the essential tasks to do that really matter. And your ONE "someday" goal is consistent with identifying your core art.

Time Blocking
In practice, The ONE Thing system accomplishes its goal by employing "time blocking," which is different from "time boxing" over several days mentioned previously. Time blocking is not a unique concept to either Keller or Less Is More--rather it is a way to execute on those.

If I had to put it in a quick elevator pitch, I'd say Less Is More is the mindset for focusing on the essential, your My One (Keller's ONE Thing) is how you can identify the essential task or directive, and time blocking is how you execute that directive.

The following diagram is an example of how this time blocking looks in a given week. It's intentionally meant to be simple and uncomplicated. If you have one of those insanely detailed, multicolored calendar situations going on, I'm not going to say it's bad. But I would like you to question if it's overkill and honestly ask yourself if it's getting in your own way.

* * *

Less Is The New More

The Less Is More Weekly View

	Sunday	Monday	Tuesday	Wednesday	Thursday	Friday	Saturday
Morning	Plan	Core Art	Core Art	Core Art	Core Art	Core Art	Core Art
Lunch							
Afternoon		Urgent not Important	Urgent not Important	Urgent not Important	Urgent not Important	Urgent not Important	
Eve		Relationships	Relationships	Relationships	Relationships	Relationships	Relationships

Summary:
Ask yourself: "What's the ONE Thing you can do such that by doing it everything else will be easier or unnecessary?"

Mental Interrupts

I majored in machine intelligence in grad school and also studied cognitive psychology. These are fields where we pretend we have the slightest clue whatsoever about the inner workings of the brain.

However, out of this study, I did develop a reasonably good theory I call "mental interrupts" which borrows an idea from computer science. I won't get too technical but here's the gist of it: In computer programming, an "interrupt" is when one computer job (program) is running and a second job cuts in (interrupts) the first one to do its job, and then lets the first one finish. The computer does this because the second job is presumably more important.

It's a little like when you're dancing, and someone cuts in to dance with your partner. It's very much like when another person interrupts you while you are in mid-sentence. In any of these cases, the presumption is that their thing is more important than yours. If your experience is anything like mine, their presumption is hardly ever valid but is instead annoying or frustrating.

"Mental interrupts" work in the same way except it is *your own brain* interrupting itself. So if another person interrupting you is frustrating, how bad is it when your own brain is doing it? It's hard to get mad at your own brain and even harder to make it stop.

Mental interrupts are the result of all those unresolved thoughts, emotions and questions you experience. Because they are unresolved, your brain will hang onto them instead of filing them away like it does when you answer a question, resolve a problem or come to terms with an emotion.

Some examples include:

- When you can't find that object you know is around here somewhere...
- When your significant other hurts you in some way, and you have no idea why
- That debate you had with someone in the comments section on the Internet when you *just must* teach them how wrong they are.
- When you're beating yourself up about the stupid thing you said to your boss, co-worker or that cute man or woman because you were flustered
- That time you were embarrassed. Actually, all those times you were embarrassed.

These mental interrupts can sit in your brain for a very long time depending on the emotional level tied to it. Any memory is more clear and persistent if it has a high level emotional attachment. So a highly emotional and unresolved experience can sit in your brain for years and causes you to eventually go crazy in some way, small or large.

Even when a mental interrupt isn't highly emotionally charged by itself, they are still debilitating because they stack up over time and keep literally interrupting your current thought process. The slightest trigger can bring one into the forefront of your mind and disrupt what you were trying to focus on. Think about that embarrassing experience you had where you had a wardrobe malfunction, or replied-all by mistake, or said something stupid in front of that cute guy/gal and thought you were going to die. And how many times have you had trouble sleeping because you were reminded of that unresolved incident and you keep replaying it in your mind--imagining what you could have said and done differently?

Part of being productive is having focus and clarity, and

to do that you must eliminate mental interrupts as much as possible. The only way to get rid of mental interrupts is to get them out of your head. Thinking about a mental interrupt just gives it more validation.

If it's an unresolved task, get it *scheduled* on paper or in your phone to-do list. Then put it out of your mind knowing you've captured it and won't forget.

It seems logical, but how many times to we forget to do this and then something keeps interrupting our train of thought ("I keep forgetting to make that appointment." "I can't forget I have to bake those cookies in two weeks."). Lots of people go as far as making a to-do list but fall short of scheduling items in the future.

If you just have a to-do list, you are faced with a big list of things your brain wants to think about. If you schedule tasks at appropriate times in the future, you can then focus on a much smaller list of to-dos (or one) for the right now. Clear your mind of interrupts and make computers--in your phone, laptop, and the Internet--deal with interrupts.

Other techniques include:

- First and foremost probably: forgive yourself. Forgive yourself for being human, and imperfect, and making mistakes and doing embarrassing things. You *will* get over most things in time. All of those embarrassing or emotional things you experienced as a teen and thought you just wanted to die--you got over them, right? At least some of them?
- Forgive other people and move on. They're human too, driven by needs and emotions and sometimes petty behaviors.
- Get it on paper. Like many things, writing it down on paper lets you think about it more objectively. Then, work on getting closure by writing down what it would take to let it go or make it go away.

***

Exercise:

Write out your mental interrupts. Name them, how they make you feel, and what would make them go away for you. You can do this exercise now, but also be aware of the mental interrupts when they pop into the forefront of your mind. If they are trivial just schedule a resolution and get back to it. If it's a less trivial issue or emotion that needs to be resolved, then spend some time with it. I'm not qualified to give you therapeutic advice, but you'll be surprised how beneficial writing something out can be, like in a journal. It helps you identify the root of the unresolved feeling, and from that, you can formulate an actionable step to rid your mind of it.

Summary:

Less Is More means eliminating those mental interrupts.

Seriously, Just Focus

As a final reference to drive home the power of focus and single-tasking, I'm going to refer to one of the world's foremost authorities on life hacking: Tim Ferriss. If you're reading this book, you're very likely to have heard of Ferriss, but in case you haven't, he is a hugely popular speaker, blogger and author of landmark books such as *The 4-Hour Workweek*[1], *The 4-Hour Body*[2] and *Tools Of Titans*[3].

Ferriss is well versed across a spectrum of life hacking areas including body, mind and work/productivity. His approach to self-improvement and life hacking is basically two-pronged:

1. He seeks out experts in the forefront and fringe of a subject area. Over the years he has managed to secure an impressive list of interviews with A-Listers from billionaires like Virgin Airlines' founder Sir Richard Branson to extreme athletes like Wim Hof.
2. He actively experiments on himself with his subject matter from mind-enhancing drugs to extreme physical regimens. He could be the poster child for "Don't try this at home, kids!"

Based on his breadth of accomplishments and experiences, Ferriss is clearly a guy who needs to--and knows how to--get things done. From Ferriss we once again find the repeated Less Is More mindset of

- Single-tasking

- Dedicating focused blocks of time to work on your priorities (or what I call core art)

Between his books, blogs and podcasts Ferriss has produced such a wealth of material that I can hardly do him justice in a small chapter. However, I will share a couple of my favorite quotes from Ferriss related to the above two principles. I give them to you verbatim and unadulterated because I find them elegant and compelling.

On single-tasking:

"First and foremost, the principle is, remembering that, single-tasking, in a digital world, is a super power--IF you cultivate it." [4]

On focused blocks of time:

"Write down the 3-5 things--and no more--that are making you most anxious or uncomfortable ... Block out at 2-3 hours to focus on ONE of them for today. Let the rest of the urgent but less important stuff slide. It will still be there tomorrow...TO BE CLEAR: Block out at 2-3 HOURS to focus on ONE of them for today. This is ONE BLOCK OF TIME. Cobbling together 10 minutes here and there to add up to 120 minutes does not work... If you get distracted or start procrastinating, don't freak out and downward spiral; just gently come back to your ONE to-do."[5]

By now you're sure to have noticed how the concept of focusing on One thing shows up repeatedly. Also, notice how Ferriss advises you to focus on tasks that take you out of your comfort zone--those that make you anxious or uncomfortable.

I can honestly and confidently say that Ferriss' book *The 4-Hour Work Week* had a profound impact on my life. I credit it for starting me along my Less Is More journey, because it made me start questioning the status quo about what success meant as well as what was really required--and more importantly what was not required--to achieve personal success.

Summary:
Yep, focus on One thing. Single-task
Also, work on things that push you out of your comfort zone.

What Would Easy Look Like?

"What would this look like if it were easy?"
Tim Ferriss

As I have discussed, Tim Ferriss has made significant contributions to the fields of personal productivity, self-improvement, and life hacking. I encourage you to explore his writings and podcast when you have the time--which you will have more of once you employ the tactics in this book (See what I did there?).

But I would like to discuss one more aspect of Ferriss' philosophy because it resonates strongly with my own Less Is More philosophy, and that is the idea that: "your reality is negotiable." I have always been fascinated when Ferriss and others are able to step back and take a look at their situation and come up with options that didn't seem to be available. It's when the "gatekeepers" and others want to maintain the status quo, try to keep you down, go through extensive rituals or "pay your dues" for long periods for no good reason. So I find it encouraging and fascinating whenever someone finds a way to go around the gatekeepers or find creative ways to shortcut a process. In other words they find a way to "negotiate" their current reality. Instead of waiting for the gatekeeper to open a gate eventually, they find or make their own gate they can open right now.

The process for identifying and creating these alternate "gateways" or options is hard to put into a formula because by definition they are always changing the current reality. I hope to write a book devoted to the subject someday, but for now we can use one particular tactic that comes from Tim Ferriss.

As explained in this article[1] (and in his writing elsewhere), Ferriss' technique is to ask the question:

"What would this look like if it were easy?"

Ferriss excels at aggressively learning what the experts do before embarking on any venture. When he set out to start his own podcast, he reached out to podcasters to learn about their experiences. One thing became clear: almost everyone who launched a podcast published about three episodes. Then they went silent. The main reason was that they would get overwhelmed by the editing process and quit.

To avoid this burnout, he thought to himself, "What would this look like if it were easy?" In this case, Ferris determined that "easy" meant no post-production work. He decided to produce long-form podcasts with long conversations and next to no editing. Wait. What? Everyone just assumed that the cumbersome post-production work was an unavoidable part of the process. By taking a step back and asking a simple but powerful question, Ferriss was able to go ahead and create a long-running, hugely successful podcast. If he had not asked himself this question, he probably would have done three episodes, then quit and moved on to something else. By questioning conventional wisdom, he was able to negotiate his reality.

And nothing (except artificial barriers) is stopping you from doing the same. It helps to close your eyes and visualize the current process and feel what aspect of your current reality is the one that most gives you that uneasy feeling in your gut or make you feel discouraged or maybe even angers you. *That* is the one you want to brainstorm on. That is the opportunity to find a way to negotiate reality.

So whatever your challenge is, try to visualize what would make it look easier:
- Can you just not do it?
- Can you simplify it significantly?
- Is there a way to accelerate it by using training or a mentor?
- Or can you find someone else to do?

Summary:
When you feel held back by anything or anyone, see if you can negotiate your reality by asking the simple but powerful question: "What would this look like if it were easy?"

Your Core Time

"Put your *core time first*, and keep it sacred."
Chris Lee, quoting himself in the 3rd person

If you get only one takeaway from this book, please let it be this one. If you read the rest of this book barely paying attention while binge-watching old Grey's Anatomy episodes on Netflix, I'm not judging you (ok, I am judging a little), but please pay attention to this one principle:

Put your *core time first*, and keep it sacred.

From a previous chapter, and after some soul searching, you should have a pretty good idea of what your *core art* is. Your *core time,* then, is simply when you work on your core art. Your core time must be made your top priority, and you must learn to find and guard it religiously.

Remember when we asked the question: "What's the ONE Thing you can do such that by doing it everything else will be easier or unnecessary?" Well, this--your core time-- is the one *principle* that makes everything easier or better for you. Once you learn to master your core time it becomes liberating in many ways. It reduces your stress level because you don't feel anxiety about not getting your priority, core art goals accomplished. Once you get your core time for yourself, you feel less resentful about the less productive non-core time. You can also use your non-core time to help others and foster your interpersonal relations.

In a way, it's similar to when a budget planner tells us to first and foremost deduct a portion of our paycheck to fund our investments. Investing for the future is an important priority so by taking out this portion first, you can put it out of your mind. Then you can deal with your mess of bills with some peace of mind knowing that you already took care of that investment priority. Similarly, when you put your priority, core art first you are *investing in yourself*. And again, you get some peace of mind knowing you took care of that first.

Of course, it's not going to be easy. In fact, it will probably be hard at first, just like it's very hard to have the discipline to take investment money out of your budget first. That's why companies have 401k investment plans to basically make you do the right thing, investment-wise.

Unfortunately, there is no 401k plan to encourage or make you pursue your passions, so you're going to have to find a way to do it yourself. Putting your core time first means making it your top priority. It also literally means trying to put it first in the day, or as early as possible. You need to get it done before low priority work and when your energy is highest (more about that later). You want to start with at least an hour every single day, and preferably work your way up to at least two hours every day. On the weekend you can shoot for four hours. As we will show in detail later, that is really not as much time as it seems.

However, I *know* it's not going to be easy. It isn't easy for me, and it's not going to be easy for most people with a typical lifestyle. But it can be done, and it will get easier. Here are some of your options for working your core time every morning:

- Get up early. Obvious--but it's also empowering. I know a lot of people aren't morning people, but I've also seen people who believed that actually go ahead and make it work. People even refer to it as joining the "5 am Club." Yes, that's a thing. It takes some time, and you're going to have to adjust your sleep schedule at the backend. In simple terms, train yourself to get to sleep earlier and then get up

earlier.
- Budget time at the beginning of your day job. I've been able to make this work just fine and still be loyal to my job--I was still putting in my 40 hours and then some. And honestly, you're not hurting your boss or co-workers. It's early, and they're still busy coming up with the next urgent-but-not-important distractions for you to do.
- If necessary park your car somewhere near your office, or park yourself at a Starbucks and get in an hour of core art before starting your workday. Of course, this won't work if your core art requires a specific physical location like a dance studio or involves chiseling on a huge chunk of granite, but for many people's projects which involve working on a laptop or with pen and paper, this works just fine.
- If your job offers flex time (adjustable hours), take advantage of it and schedule some core time between your home life and work day.
- Use that lunch hour. Take the *full* hour and forget, for an hour, all the other things you need to get done. Also, see if you can take your lunch break a little early. By noon you've already used up a lot of your energy and freshness, but it's still in the first half and way better than doing nothing towards your core art. If you combine a full lunch hour with one of the other options you have found at least two hours of core time.

Again, I know this is not going to be easy, especially at first, but it can be done, and you only need one of the above options to start. If all else is not an option, getting up early is going to be your "jam." Embrace it and ease into it. Once you decide how to schedule your core time, stick to it and guard it religiously. You may feel guilty at first but there is absolutely no reason you should. You are going to spend a ton of the rest of your day doing things for other people. And sometimes we put the limitation on ourselves. Once we train people to respect our schedule, they are usually fine with it.

Summary:
Put your core time first.

Todo List

- [x] My One
- [ ] other
- [ ] less
- [ ] important
- [ ] stuff

Affirmation

I believe that a self-help or personal transformation book should focus on actionable advice, or at least should not just be filled cover to cover with feel-good, cheer-leading advice. So I've refrained from too much motivational talk and tried instead to motivate you with tactics you will feel like you can actually use.

I am going to make an exception in this chapter on "Affirmation." Even then I am intentionally speaking about one affirmation (singular) instead of "affirmations" (plural). To clarify, I mean one affirmation verse consisting of multiple lines of affirmation which you can easily remember. In any case, I believe a concise and relevant affirmation done once a day *can* be truly motivational and help keep you on the path to success and accomplishment. I also said in the introduction that I want you to embrace a Less Is More *mindset*, and a good affirmation can help you greatly with this.

A good affirmation should be worded like it is *already happening*--not in the future. If you try to do it in the future tense, you are programming your mind to have the same mindset as you already have now. *Someday* is the same as *never going to happen*.

So you must use the present tense to tell your mind it is happening. Otherwise you will train your mind to believe success is always in the future. There is one issue with this though: when you first start doing the affirmation, your mind will say to itself "liar" and brings up all those doubts you have. That's why it's hard to start by affirming something like "I am a rock star!" Your mind knows you're not a rock star, and it will link what you are saying to self-doubt instead of self-confidence and just reinforce all your insecurities.

But there is a way to make this work: if you say something like "I am *becoming* a rock star!"--well, that has truth to it. You are starting a journey of change, right here, right now with your affirmation.

At first your mind will reluctantly believe it. But because there is a seed of truth, your mind will tell itself: "ok, I can get behind this." Over time, and with each tiny success, your mind will believe it more strongly.

Other variations include things like:

- "I am becoming more and more of X every day."
- "I am crushing Y..." This is legit and inspirational because you can start crushing anything today.
- "It's amazing how I am becoming Z ..."

Here is a checklist of tips to create good affirmations:

- Start with the words "I am," or "My," or "Every day I."
- Use the present tense, not the future.
- Always word it in the positive form: what you want, not what you don't.
- Make it specific if you can.
- Tie it to a powerful emotional word or verb, not a weak one.
- Include an action verb, like "crushing."
- Make it centered on *your* growth and behavior, not what others ask of you which you can't easily control.

I said I advocated *one* affirmation verse, and so I think it's ok to mix in your core "being" goals with your "doing" goals. Obviously with a Less Is More mindset you shouldn't include every possible life goal in your affirmation. It should focus on your current core art and goals and you can, and should, modify your affirmation over time to focus on your current priorities.

If you don't do some kind of affirmation, you deny your mind the opportunity to recognize and internalize the progress you are making.

Summary:

Write one good affirmation, focused on your current priorities, and repeat it to yourself every day on waking and/or before going to sleep.

An example affirmation:

Every day I express my gratitude for the gifts I have!
I am embracing a mindset of abundance!
I am crushing my Spanish learning program!
I am conquering my anxiety, I am defeating it steadily each day.
I am becoming (insert disease or condition)-free! My immune system is healthy, strong, and protecting me right now!
I am becoming a world-class motivational coach!

LESS Multitasking Actions

1. Block out your core time and put your core art first.
2. Focus on your My One: the One thing you can do now that will make everything else easier or unnecessary.
3. Use the 80/20 principle to identify the tasks that will accomplish the most value with the least effort.
4. Eliminate mental interrupts.
5. When faced with a challenging task, ask yourself: "What would easy look like?"
6. Make one affirmation focused on your priorities and say it to yourself every day.

LESS Distractions

Why Do I Care?

"Why do I care?" This question is not only relevant to your Less Is The New More mindset, but could be applied to this entire book, or even to your life in general. But I am putting it in this LESS Distractions section, because it is especially critical for learning how to eliminate distractions in your work and life.

In order to embrace this new mindset, you need to train yourself to constantly ask yourself "Why do I care?" about this. This is *not* the same as saying "I don't care." This is not meant to turn you into an uncaring person. Rather it is meant to make you think a little more proactively and teach yourself to only care about what is really important, and forgetting or eliminating everything else, or least as much as you can.

Don't care about unimportant things.

Shortly, in the section *Important versus Urgent* chapter, I'm going to go into detail about how you define what you should care about versus what you should not care about, or care less about.

However, I have also talked about how critical it is to prioritize your core art first. So when you ask yourself "Why do I care?" you should also be asking "Is this important to my core art and goals?" If not, then you need to care less about doing them.

Don't care what people think about you.

Aside from caring too much about doing tasks that aren't really important about us, we often expend effort because we care what other people think about us. Of course you should care about things like your job performance and giving good customer service but it's easy to take this too far and do work simply because we have an emotional need to care too much about what unimportant people think of us.

This is another one of those things that's easy to say but hard to do. It's hard to make yourself stop feeling something.

However, one powerful psychological tactic that you can use is, instead of trying to eliminate your emotional reaction, learn to *replace it with a different one.* This works more effectively than trying not to have a response. And one way to do this is:

Care what other people feel.

In other words, think about their motivations and care about how you affect them instead of letting them affect you. Don't care about your pride--or conversely--let them make you feel bad about yourself. You keep the control inside yourself, and keep the negativity outside and learn to keep yourself more detached from your decision about how to proceed. If their motivation is weak or suspicious, you won't feel bad turning down their request. Even if their motivation is something like jealousy, you can feel sorry for them in a small way, but you have refused to let them bring you down. And you are detached from that negativity.

When you shift the focus away from how other people make you feel to thinking about what *they* are feeling, and what is driving their behavior, you can start to take the higher ground. (Look at you being all grown up!) You can start to understand their motivations and empathize with them. Or if it's not a behavior you want to condone, you can figure out how to respond more calmly and objectively, and not as a knee-jerk reaction. The result will be to improve the quality of your interactions and relationships. Or in some cases it will mean removing toxic relationships.

In any case, it reduces that anxiety from your life.

Summary:
Actively learn when to care, and what to care about. And when and what not to care about. LESS is MORE is liberating.

Important Versus Urgent

The next principle I want to discuss is called the "Eisenhower Decision Principle," and the system is referred to as the "Eisenhower Matrix." If you haven't heard this before it's worth talking about and if you have, it's worth reviewing from the perspective of Less Is More.

This principle is attributed to US President Dwight D. Eisenhower:

"I have two kinds of problems, the urgent and the important. The urgent are not important, and the important are never urgent."[1]

Even if you don't know it by name, if you work with or for—well, anyone—you are familiar with that feeling that sometimes, or much of the time, you are scrambling to complete work that is "urgent" for someone else, but for you—not so much.

The Difference Between Urgent and Important

Urgent tasks are those that require immediate attention. These are often things needed by other people or things that have negative consequences associated with them. They are further associated with a feeling or mindset of being defensive (covering your butt), feeling rushed, and focused on short-term thinking (I don't care how this affects tomorrow, I want this now).

Important tasks are things that contribute to your core values and core art—your long-term projects and goals. Important tasks seldom get the urgent attention because of their tendency to be long term projects (we can get to that later). So they continually get pre-empted by the urgent tasks.

And that is a problem for two reasons:

1. It causes us stress because we feel like really important goals are getting postponed, maybe forever, and
2. Working on important tasks is associated with the feeling and mindset of accomplishment and being proactive which helps us remain calm, rational, and open to exploring options and opportunities.

	URGENT	NOT URGENT
IMPORTANT	Do	Decide
NOT IMPORTANT	Delegate	Delete

How do we use this information? That's where the Eisenhower Matrix comes in and is used as a decision matrix for action. As shown, the matrix has four quadrants with two dimensions:

1. Important vs. Not Important, and
2. Urgent vs. Not Urgent.

The matrix works by simply taking your extended to-do list of tasks and assigning them to the appropriate quadrants in the matrix. You can't just use your daily to-do list because consciously or unconsciously that probably won't contain much in the way of strategic long-term goals or tasks. You need to consider (not necessarily do) a mix of immediate tasks (today, this week) as well as long term goals (year goals, for example).

Now armed with the knowledge of where the tasks fall in the matrix, you use the quadrants to decide how to proceed, as follow:

Quadrant 1: Important and urgent. These are tasks that should be done immediately, and further should be handled by you personally because they are crises, deadlines or problems that have consequences to you and your long term goals.

Quadrant 2: Important but not urgent. These are also important to your long term goals and values and should be done by you personally. But since they are not urgent, they should be planned, prioritized, and scheduled to be done at the appropriate time to accomplish your goals. This also includes setting aside time for things like physical fitness and relationships.

Quadrant 3: Not important but urgent. These are tasks that are not important to you but may be a challenge to avoid because they are important to someone else, which could be your superior, customer, family or friends. You can reduce the impact of these by minimizing, delegating or sometimes ignoring them. Some tasks you can determine are not needed or have a workaround (ignore). Some can be negotiated (minimized) or compromised in some way with the other party. And for any of them, see if there is someone you can delegate or outsource it too.

Quadrant 4: Not important and not urgent.
These are blatant time-wasters that should be dropped, including doing someone else's unimportant or unappealing grunt work. Others in this category include recreational activities like watching TV and surfing social media that do little or nothing to improve your core art, physical fitness or relationships (if you are being honest). If you are going to do these, that's fine but you need to aggressively manage when and how long you do them.

Summary:
Focus on a balance of important tasks in Quadrant 1 and Quadrant 2. Minimize, delegate and ignore tasks in Quadrants 3 and (especially) 4.

Take Back Ownership Of Your Time

I'm not sure who first said this, or which 10 other people I also read or heard say it, but it's a popular saying because it's absolutely true:

"If you don't schedule your time, someone else will."

Further, when they schedule your time it will usually not be for something you want to do or your core priorities, but instead will be for something *they* want or need you to do (mostly want). These include things like:

- Asking you to do tasks they could do themselves but don't want to.
- They are scheduling endless meetings that help them achieve their agenda but only serve to distract you from working on your core art and priorities.
- Scheduling social commitments with people you don't much care about.

So if you don't take back ownership of your time, others will *gladly* fill that vacuum for you. I am not naive enough or unrealistic to suggest that you can get out of all possible commitments, or that you should totally cut others out of your life (though there may be some toxic people you should consider cutting out completely). I know you can't tell your boss that you won't do any of her requests. And you shouldn't neglect the needs of your relationship with co-workers, friends, and family. But to put it bluntly, stop letting them walk all over you. Help make your relationship with your boss and co-workers a beneficial and productive two-way street. Strive to create smaller periods of quality time with spouse, family, and friends and they should respect and value you for it.

Other sections will cover more specific tactics on how to reclaim your own time, but here are some easy ones:

- First: block out time for your core art. This is one of the biggest bangs for the buck because it will make you less stressed and frustrated with everything and everyone else.
- Block out appointments for yourself. At work, block them out on your calendar.
- At home, tell your significant other and/or kids that you will gladly do X with them at Y time, but right now you will be doing Z. And then honor your commitment, and they will respect you for it
- When the requests are reasonable, be transparent and communicate with others about when you can get to their request, but not how. This is often all they need to know—that you will get to their request in a timely manner, not immediately.

On the other hand, you are under no obligation to be transparent about your goals or priorities. Nor do you have to make excuses for not dropping what you are doing to work on their request. Clearly there will be times when you must do that, but make sure they are truly urgent. Otherwise, work on training others, and yourself, that you will manage your own time. You don't have to say this out loud, just work on taking control of your schedule, step by step. They will figure it out, and you will start to internalize it.

Summary:
Reclaim ownership of your time.

Email: The Great Distractor

If you want to get more done, you're going to have to spend time—probably way less time—reading and answering email. You may be thinking to yourself "Really Chris? That is your great advice? Everyone knows this. It's mentioned in every 'getting things done' book since the dawn of email".

True, but there's a reason it's on every productivity coach's "not to do" list, and that's because it's The Great Distractor and one of the biggest time wasters, especially in your day job. And your day job represents a big chunk of your day. If you don't get control of email, you're not going to get very far in your quest to get more done. You have to tackle this like a linebacker. A linebacker is a position on an American football team. If you are not familiar with this term, that's ok—just be assured that a linebacker is someone who is very good at tackling things.

We all know that social media in general can be a huge time waster, and email is basically the longest lasting form of social media. It's double jeopardy because it impacts your personal productivity as well as almost certainly impacting your work productivity.

Some forms of social media come and go, but email refuses to go away and continues to be important to almost every business. Your goal is *not* to get rid of it—it's to apply the Less Is The New More mindset to make it work for you and not against you.

One reason you read email is that you don't know what

to be doing next, or you *do* know what you should be doing next and it's something you don't want to do. It makes sense: if you don't feel like doing some challenging or distasteful task, start reading and answering emails. Your boss can fault you for responding to your emails, right? However he can fault you for not getting done those things you are avoiding. So at the risk of repeating other productivity experts' advice, I will give you some things you can do to get control of your email.

The first and most important thing you must do is to limit the number of times you check email per day. Two to four times a day should be the maximum you shoot for. As far as what time of day you should check email is probably a decision best left to you and your situation. However, I would strongly recommend not doing email first thing in the morning—defer it until just before lunch (preferably) or at least later in the morning. Why? Because you're going to prioritize your core art first, and your important-versus-urgent tasks.

At this point you may be angrily saying: "There's no way I can do this at my job!" I emphatically argue that most people can, and here are some reasons why:

Very few emails are really so urgent they can't wait a few hours.

People send emails to get them off their mind or to-do list and go about doing something else, not expecting an immediate reply.

And last but not least, there are actually days when I can process my email *zero* times. How is that possible? Because people frequently contact me in some other way when the email topic is actually urgent. I can't tell you how many times this conversation has happened:

* * *

A co-worker (in person): "Hey, did you see my email?"

Me: "Sorry, no, I was [in meeting such-and-such or doing some legit task]. When did you send it?"

Co-worker: "A few minutes ago. It's about ...[proceed to tell me all I need]".

So I did not actually need to open that email at all. Of course if they abuse interrupting me in person that's another problem, but my point is if it's really urgent I will certainly find out about it without opening my email.

Note: *You do not have to declare* to others that you are only reading email twice a day. You just need to train them to realize you aren't checking it every five minutes.

Here are some other tips:
- Only look at the top of the email chain. Maybe this seems obvious, but some people like to scroll way back to their first unread email and start sequentially going through them. This is unnecessary because many emails are chains and the latest one has all the information so far.
- Resists the urge to always respond. Sometimes the sender figures out the answer while they are waiting for you to respond. If the email is CC'd to others, sometimes they will respond.
- Apply the "4 Hour Rule," or sometimes even the "3 Day Rule" to your email. Sometimes a request is a random idea the other person had and it won't actually go any further. They usually won't tell you that however, and you might spend an hour or more researching an answer. Use your judgment, but if

you wait several hours or a few days to see if they bring up the request again. If not, assume you may never hear about the idea or request again.
- Actively use filters in your email program to remove noise from your mailbox. You can use filters to take out spammy emails you hardly ever pay attention to, and you can use other filters to categorize your emails. As with many other areas of productivity, anything you can automate is a win.

Summary:
Manage your email, or it will manage you.

Minimize the One-Offs

Scott Adams is the creator of the famous comic strip: "Dilbert" which captures, in sometimes eerie accuracy, the reality of cubicle life as an engineer at a technology company. In 1996 Adams' book "The Dilbert Principle" was published. The book mixed select episodes of his comic strip interspersed with Adams' business observations based on the trials and tribulations of his work in the technology and business sectors. He also drew from a wealth of comments and feedback he received from readers of his comic strip. Adams has commented that he draws inspiration from actual cubicle workers who were readers of his strip. Once his comic strip started gaining popularity it resonated so well with the daily grind and frustrations of white-collar workers, that people were sending him examples of how his satirical episodes mirrored what they were experiencing in their jobs. I was working at Motorola, a telecom icon at the time, and I would bet serious money that at least a couple of the Dilbert strip jokes were based on actual management decisions at Motorola.

I still consider The Dilbert Principle one of my favorite books on management. Unlike other management books, it did not preach on the feel-good management initiatives being used at successful companies. Instead it focused on the various ways in which management at large companies went astray from sound business principles, personal relationships and sometimes plain common sense.

One principle Adams presented which I thought was particularly brilliant and insightful was the concept of "one-offs," and it is something that has stuck with me throughout the years. Adams didn't use the hyphen in "one-off" but I will use one so I don't have to keep using quotes.

Adams defined a one-off as *any activity at least one level removed from something that improves either the effectiveness of the people or the quality of the product.*

If you're testing a better way to assemble a product, that's fundamental. But if you're working on a *task force* to develop a *suggestion system* then you're one level removed.

Other examples of one-offs in business include:

- Process Improvement
- Status reports
- Standards
- Policy improvement
- Reorganization
- Budget processes
- Writing Mission Statements

You can easily find other examples of one-offs in your own company and see how many activities are at least one level removed. Please understand, none of these are particularly bad by themselves and some are necessary or even required by legal regulations and compliance. The problem is the more they stack up, the more time is taken away from the company's real value in its product and people.

In Adams' blunt assessment: "Any activity that is one level removed from your people or your product will ultimately fail or have little benefit. It won't seem like that when you're doing it, but it's a consistent pattern." That may seem harsh, but many of you have been there and experienced the endless stream of initiatives that distract you from doing your core job.

Let's consider, for a minute, the benefit versus cost

(including time and effort) with a few examples:

- Status reports--a historical pet peeve of mine. Countless hours spent on telling management what they should already know or can be better communicated with one-on-one communication.
- Employee satisfaction surveys. Are simply lip service and wasted time if no significant followup changes are made.
- Mission and Vision statements can be highly effective for polarizing an organization. However, I can think of maybe one mission statement in my career that had clarity and wasn't so vague and generic that it couldn't have come from any other company or department.

The one-off problem does not just apply to cubicle life; the same problem applies to your own entrepreneurial and personal life:

- Making a to-do list is technically a one-off compared to actually getting the task done. Yes, I still make to-do lists but I keep the process dead simple and fast.
- Reading a bunch of *blog posts* about how to make the best to-do list would be a "two-off."
- Let's agree that having a calendar is pretty important for not missing appointments and soccer games. However, spending hours managing an elaborate colored calendar is a one-off.
- Creating that fancy dream board and other feng shui activities to help motivate you and get you in the "zone."
- Reading a self-improvement book about "getting things done" is a one-off as compared to actually doing a thing.

* * *

Again I'm *not suggesting* you don't do any of these things. (Especially the last one—please don't stop reading this book.) You just need to be aware of what work is directly spent on your core art and self-improvement, and what is a one-off. The more time you spend on your one-offs means less time you are spending on what really matters.

Action Item:
- Make a One-off worksheet with two columns.
- In the left column, identify items you do at work or home.
- In the right column labels them as "core art" or "one-offs."

Your mission, if you choose to accept it, is to maximize time spent on your core art and minimize time spent on one-offs.

Summary:
Minimize the one-offs, two-offs and N-offs. Focus on your core art.

A Typical Work Day

Here is an example work day that clearly illustrates the problem. This example was taken from one of my real work days; on Monday, October 22, 2018, to be exact:

- I had *eight* meetings already on my calendar, some of them overlapping. A couple more meetings were requested.
- I had at least 10 new email requests from people by 9am wanting help with questions or issues. One was a request from someone who wanted me to prep for, and attend, a meeting—basically to do her job for her, to help *her* project.
- Meanwhile I was in the last critical week of my own high visibility project. However, almost no-one was going to help me with my own project.
- But wait, there's more: add in the usual people wanting to stop me in the hallway.
- Even during the lunch period--the only open slot I had all day, a data scientist wanted to engage in an extended discussion with me.

I am not telling you this to impress you with how busy I am. Because first of all, I consider it an embarrassment and a failure on my part to let my situation get that out of control. Also I know that many, many of you have similar days whether you are corporate workers, small business owners or stay-at-home parents.

The old me would have rushed between all the meetings. And tried to respond to all the emails immediately—probably while in meetings—and not giving my full attention to the discussion at hand. Then at the end of the day I would have responded to any remaining semi-urgent requests. If I was lucky I would have a few moments to work on my own project. More likely I would have to rush home (late) and be bitter and stressed that I had zero time for my own project.

So what did I do instead?

- First, I spent a productive hour, before anything else, working on my own project. Even one hour of quality time spent on *your* priority needs can be game-changing.
- I declined a couple of meetings. By doing this I carved out more time to work on my project team's needs.
- I refused to look at my email until the end of the morning. Not surprisingly, some issues got managed without me.
- I *chose* to attend a particular meeting, because that person had in fact helped my project. This was different because it was my choice to attend and it was consistent with my integrity to return the favor.
- The hallway stops? Usually I would say I was on my way to a meeting but would get in touch later (which I would "forget" to do).
- For the manager who wanted me to do her work? I sent one of my developers in my place--someone she didn't like to work with. It may not have been the most mature thing on my part but it was oh so satisfying.

By employing this variety of techniques, I could carve out a big chunk of my day to work on My One priority project. This was sufficient to get plenty of productive work done and then I could spend the rest of my time on the other urgent-but-less-important items. Some of these came from my senior management, or from my other teams, so it wasn't feasible to ignore them. But by prioritizing My One, I was less stressed, didn't have to stay late, and ultimately got more work done that actually mattered across the board.

Defer Social Media

Many books and articles have been written lately about the need to stop using social media in order to increase your productivity. In other news, many books have *also* been written advising on the importance of using social media extensively to market your brand or business. So who do you listen to? The answer is probably "both." It's an incredible time to be alive in the age of the Internet, and entrepreneurs and artists have never had a more powerful tool at their literal fingertips.

However, I'm sure you will also agree that social media can be an incredibly addictive time-waster. I'm not going to get on a soapbox or get judge-y because I've been there and done that. Instead, I'll just share what I found to be some of the better tactics for keeping your social media habit under control.

Stop being available 24/7

You need to train everyone else, and especially yourself, that you will not be available during all your waking hours to notice everyone's last post in real time or even respond to their texts. You need to break the hold your smartphone has on you. I understand it is not actually your phone that you're addicted to--it is just the messenger. The real addiction is the access to an entire planet of people like yourself (or wonderfully different) that you can connect to and interact with, which is why the addiction is so powerful. I mean c'mon--a portal to a planet of people in the palm of your hand?

There are many aspects of the allure to social media,

but I would say a main reason we are so addicted to it is because of FOMO (Fear Of Missing Out). Now that we know all those wonderful posts and social interactions are out there, we don't want to miss out on *anything*. But here are a few things to consider:

- You *are* going to miss out on things: conversations, threads, and memes. There is way too much going on, on the Web, and even in your own timeline for you to keep up with it all. Trying to do so is going to drive you crazy.
- There is very little information on social media that is of such high importance that you need to respond immediately or can't live without. It's sufficient to follow certain friends, influencers or groups, and checking your updates a few times a day will do the trick. Also, those cute cat videos aren't going anywhere, and besides, your online friends are going to repost them 1,000 times anyway so you are not going to miss out.
- Any real friends are not going to unfollow or disown you because they don't see you online hourly or if you don't respond to their messages immediately.

To avoid wasting too much time due to your FOMO and social media addiction, I would strongly advise you to take your cell phone offline for periods, at least during your core time. Only go online if there's a specific important task that you absolutely need to do on your cell phone. Oh, My, God you're thinking--did he just say that? How can I possibly be offline and disconnected from the world? You can, and you need to. Your circumstances will vary, and you are going to have to use your judgment as to how you will disconnect, depending on how you need to be available for *true* emergencies:

- First, just train yourself to be disciplined. It *is*

possible.
- Use airplane mode or another setting on your phone to disconnect for a while
- Use an app. There are apps designed to block distractions by keeping you from going online for a period of time. A couple of them are Freedom[1] and Cold Turkey Blocker[2]. Check them out.

Mini-sabbaticals

You *can* use these tactics, and life *will* go on--both in the social media world and in the real world (which will actually benefit from your presence). You can *also* make this more fun and treat it like mini-sabbaticals from social media. Actually I encourage you to take longer social media sabbaticals of a long weekend (baby steps), a week, or even longer. You will benefit from it personally, and you may actually strengthen your online relationships. You can use it as a topic of discussion on your own social media. Your true friends or even decent followers will still be there for you on your return. I have personally taken long breaks from social media and received a warm welcome back.

Quality Vs. Quantity

Another thing you can do to help corral your social media time is to focus on quality interactions. You don't have to feel compelled to comment on every cute cat video and (for the love of God) don't feel like you have to comment on any political comment. The latter will just send you down a rabbit hole of trolling, unsupported opinions and debate.

Instead, you should focus on quality interactions, both by yourself and others. You don't have to post 10 times a day and you don't need to follow everyone. By "follow" I am not talking about when you click "Follow" on Twitter and Instagram. You can follow as many people as you like, but I am advising that you only "follow" (as in reading regularly) the activities of some key influencers or friends. In other words, no matter how many people you follow or are followed by, focus on a small set of quality interactions and relationships. You can casually relate to others.

Schedule it

Ok, but what if social media is a legitimate, required aspect of your business or brand? You need to interact regularly to keep up our brand and relationship with customers and fans. Well, first of all, the tips above still apply and will be helpful. But you still need to manage the time you spend in any given day or week, or it will kill your productivity. So, just like with email, you need to try and schedule your social media. I know that sounds counter-intuitive and not much fun, but it's something you're going to need to try and do. Those posts will still be there waiting for you later, but you will save a lot of time and be much more efficient if you restrict your social media activity (in general at least) to once or twice a day *and* limit the amount of time you spend in any social media session. No, "day" and "night" do not count as only two times a day.

You can limit your social media interactions in this way and still have a high quality social media presence. In fact, you might improve your presence (quality over quantity again).

Jot and do later

The other distraction you're going to run into is when you are trying to focus on your core art, and you keep thinking of things you need to look up on the Web. This may not just be social media specifically, but could include things you want to Google on the web for research in some way. Even if it is for legitimate research purposes, I urge you to resist the impulse to open a browser at that point. Instead you should keep a "jot list." This could be on pen and paper if that's what you have handy or an electronic list if you have one that is easy and very quick to make an entry into. So when the urge to browse pops in your head--whether it be work-related or anything else--just quickly jot it down and move on. That way you don't lose what may actually be a valuable idea but you won't derail your work at the moment. Then later, at your scheduled social media time, you can go to your list of those things you jotted down and google or pursue them as you want.

This is also known as "batching" your social media tasks. Instead of constantly going back and forth between your other work and social media, you can do both more efficiently by focusing on them in their time.

Summary:
Only connect with social media at planned times.
Focus on the quality, not the quantity of interactions
Use a system to jot down social media tasks to do later.

The Art Of the Graceful "No"

"Essentialism is not about how to get more things done, it's about how to the get the right things done."
Greg McKeown

Greg McKeown is an author who squarely fits in with the Less Is More philosophy. He calls his philosophy "Essentialism." He may not have invented the Essentialism philosophy but he clearly and effectively drives it home in his book *Essentialism: The Disciplined Pursuit of Less*.[1] His principles very much align with my own experience and if you are interested in reading more I can highly recommend his book.

I could dedicate an entire section to McKeown's philosophy, but instead I will just cover his pillars and then expand on one section I found particularly helpful, which is his advice on how to effectively say "no." To take it a step further, he offers specific advice on what he calls 'The Art Of The Graceful "No."'

The purpose of the Graceful No is to give you a polite way to say "no" to people when they are trying to get you to do work you don't need, want or shouldn't be doing. This may be work that is urgent-but-not-important ,or it may be work that they don't want to do themselves and are therefore trying to get you to do. And finally, it may be important work delegated or assigned by your superior, but which is going to disrupt what you are currently doing or add too much work to your already overloaded plate. In all these situations you may realize you shouldn't be taking on the new task. But you feel uncomfortable saying "no" because you're a people pleaser, you don't want to make waves, or you don't want to get fired or get a bad review. But there are ways to say no and still stay in your comfort zone.

But before we talk about *how* to do this, let's briefly review the importance of *why* you need to do this. Essentialism, like Less Is More, generally looks for ways to eliminate, minimize or delegate tasks in order to reclaim time to work on important tasks. The Graceful No is focused on the *eliminate* principle. It's important to learn how to say no to incoming tasks, or you will never free up enough core time to focus on your core art. So the first thing you want to do with this is to get clear on your reason for saying no by thinking about these things:

- Be really clear about your purpose. Remind yourself of your core art, principles and goals.
- Learn to ask yourself: what will I say "no" to? With your core art, principles and goals in mind, anything else becomes a candidate for saying "no" to. That may seem extreme, but it's the base assumption you should start with. If it doesn't further my core art, principles or goals it should be a "no."
- *Important note: If you have balanced principles and goals you will not be selfish by doing this, because you have included room for relationships with others in your principles and goals.*
- So to summarize: eliminate any activity that is misaligned with what you want to achieve.

Some other points to consider:

- You don't actually have to use the word "no" if it makes you uncomfortable. At least not always—you should still learn to get comfortable with saying no.

- Remind yourself of the trade-off of not saying no. Are you really hurting the situation by saying "yes" instead of speaking up when you know you should?
- Saying no involves trading popularity for respect. By always saying "yes" you are ultimately giving up your respect. Shouldn't you give up some of your popularity (or appearing a nice person) to keep your respect?
- A clear no is better than a vague yes. If you say yes to a task that you won't get done or will be late, or of shoddy quality, then you aren't helping anyone.

And with no further ado, here are some of the ways offered by McKeown that you can use to say a Graceful No:

The No Repertoire:

- *Use the awkward pause. This can actually be a fun one. Just pause for a few seconds. The person asking you to do the task will often be put on the defensive and try to fill in the awkward silence. They will start to second guess the legitimacy of their request. At the very least, it puts them on notice that you are not a pushover.*

- *The " no, but..." In this case you are refusing the request, but offering a legitimate explanation (not an apology—you don't need that) why you won't do the task. You may offer a legitimate reason why not, someone else to do it, or something else they can do instead.*

- *"Let me check my calendar and get back to you." This lets you avoid saying "yes" because they put you on the spot. It also reminds the requester that "guess what, I have a full calendar with a bunch of my own work to do."*

- *Use email bounce-backs. For requests coming by email. In most email programs like Outlook, you can set up rules to automatically respond to an email and say in some way you are busy and won't be responding to their request at this time.*

- *Say yes, but "What should I de-prioritize?" This is appropriate for responding to a superior. Chances are you are already doing multiple important assignments for them, and so this reminds them of that and makes them pick the one or two that are most important to them. One or two—not all of them and one more.*

- *Say it with humor. You can say something like "You're kidding right? Have you seen my backlog?" or "Yeah, that's not going to happen." The idea is to casually dismiss their request as if to say they couldn't really be serious and politely wish them the best. Again you're not apologizing. Some people can do this more naturally than others, but it's still a tactic that's usable by most people. If they keep pushing you can say "I seriously thought you were joking," and more firmly state your position that you will not do the task.*

- *Say you are welcome to X, I am willing to do Y. In other words, you still tell them "no," but you are softening the blow and being helpful by offering or negotiating alternatives.*

- *I can't do it, but X (person) might be interested. This is fairly self-explanatory. Maybe there is someone else who is more appropriate, willing or eager to fulfill the task.*

Summary:
- Learn The Art of the Graceful No to eliminate unwanted tasks being dropped on you but with less potential confrontation.

LESS Distractions Actions

1. Focus on your important versus urgent tasks.
2. Reclaim ownership of your time.
3. Manage your email, or it will manage you.
4. Minimize the one-offs
5. Only connect with social media at planned times.
6. Learn The Art Of The Graceful "No."

LESS Barriers

Less Friction

If "LESS Multitasking" and "LESS Distractions" are important for starting projects and getting things done, then having "LESS Barriers" is critical for not giving up and actually finishing projects. Also, it's time to be honest with ourselves and admit that minimizing friction often means minimizing the **excuses** we make for ourselves.

In fact, I was thinking about naming this section of the book "LESS Excuses" instead of "LESS Barriers". However, that seemed a little heavy-handed and judge-y. And while I believe we do make excuses, productive and well-meaning people also experience a lot of legit other barriers to getting things done.

One of the keys to removing barriers is minimizing "friction". What is friction? Personally I'm not a big fan of when an author whips out some stuffy dictionary or Wikipedia definition, which usually leaves the reader scratching their head and thinking: "huh?" So I'm going to give you the practical, street-friendly definition:

Friction is anything that slows you down, or keeps you from starting or moving in the first place, or makes you come to a stop.

We don't want any of those things to happen, which is why it's important to minimize friction. Think of friction as a guiding mindset principle, one that could be applied to any of the first three pillars of this book: LESS Multitasking, LESS Distractions, and LESS Barriers. So, as you are choosing and acting on tactics in this book to improve and simplify your life, think about how they can reduce friction:

- What friction (task) can you defer (less multitasking) to let you get started and focus on your highest priority, your My One?
- What friction (distractions) are slowing you down and keeping you from spending enough time on your priority, your My One thing?
- What friction (barriers) are causing you to fizzle out and stop completing what you started?

The Hemingway Method

Here is a *less friction* tactic to get you started.

The Famous American author and journalist Ernest Hemingway would stop his day's work in the middle of a sentence, so he knew where to start in the morning.[1]

That's counterintuitive, yes? If you're like me, from birth (or maybe while in the womb), you've been told, coached or lectured to finish what you start. That's absolutely what we want to do in the long run, but what a powerful tactic this represents in the short run, to help you finish in the long run. And this is from the prolific, legendary writer Hemingway no less.

Everybody understands that *friction* is a killer of productivity, even if they don't call it that. Getting started on a task you know you need to do can be incredibly difficult some days because you literally don't know where to start. Also, as far as I've seen, experts on productivity agree unanimously that if you can just find a way to get started you will start to get in the zone and productivity will follow.

You don't have to be a writer like Hemingway to use this tactic. Here are some ideas:

For that business proposal you are working on, stop in the middle of a sentence in your document.

Similarly, for that (core priority) PowerPoint presentation you need to finish, make a slide and leave it half finished as a place to pick up first thing tomorrow. That way you don't have to think twice about where to pick up.

Make a note to yourself as a place to pick up tomorrow.

I do this all the time for myself, including when I was writing this book. I do something like this:

- I use square brackets and the word "TODO" so I can search and find them all later.
- If you're writing computer code, just stop in the middle of a command. The compiler will point out exactly what you need to work on next (lame inside programmer joke).
- If you're writing a speech, don't worry—you are probably already stuck in the middle of a sentence. Put that half-thought down on paper or computer and dive in tomorrow with a fresh mind.

These may seem like simplistic ideas, but when it comes to getting things done, there is sometimes nothing worse or more paralyzing than staring at a blank page.

What other ideas can you think of to stop "midway" and then have a no-brainer, frictionless way to quickly dive into your work later, or tomorrow?

Summary: Use the Hemingway Method to reduce friction.

Accountability Is Key

Accountability is a key driver for success and, not surprisingly, I'll state it's also key for the Less Is More mindset. In a study done by the American Society of Training and Development, now known as ATD: the Association for Talent Development[1], they found that people are 65 percent likely to meet a goal after committing to another person. Their chances of success increase to 95 percent when they build in ongoing meetings with their partners to check in on their progress.

Self-discipline is an important factor for achieving anything in life. However, there is a limit to how much you can achieve with sheer willpower. Even the most disciplined people will run out of motivation at times, and for many of us, maintaining discipline is not our strongest quality. In my opinion, a lot of creative and entrepreneurial people struggle in this area because we (I include myself) get distracted frequently by new inspirations and creative ideas.

That's why many successful people use external help to make sure they're staying on track when they run out of willpower. For Olympic and professional athletes it's a given that a *coach* is needed, not just for technical advising but to provide constant motivation during those low periods in the long journey of hard, demanding work. There is no reason it should be different in the business or art world and in fact more and more executives and professionals are hiring coaches for mentorship, and also for motivation and accountability.

Almost any achievement is completed as a result of accountability. The accountability may come from your employer, family, society or yourself. The last one--making yourself accountable--is the most critical one when it comes to self-improvement and achieving your personal goals. I don't want to be negative here, but the fact is no-one else ultimately cares about your goals except you. Sure, you can get some support from friends, family or support groups but they will be focused on their own needs.

So accountability is a must for consistently achieving your goals and completing your core art projects. As mentioned, like executives, you could hire your own personal coach, and these days, personal coaches are very much in vogue and a single Google search will return more coaches than you know what to do with. It will also guarantee that ads for coaches will pop up all over your web pages until the end of time. However they don't come cheaply, and I get that. Fortunately, you have a variety of options for accountability:

Use a personal coach on a limited basis. I don't want to give you the impression that I am anti-coach; I just understand that it can be a big investment of time or you may be hesitant to make such a commitment. Fortunately, you can find coaches that offer limited sessions and can do it via Skype or other convenient methods.

Find a mentor. In contrast to a coach, a mentor is someone who doesn't charge for advice as a business but is willing to give back to others by sharing their experience. Because they are not charging for their time you need to approach them carefully, ease into any relationship, and not abuse their valuable time and benevolent nature. You will have to decide who in your field or life may be a candidate for being a mentor, but don't discount people you think might be out of your reach. Also, the best mentor relationships are a two-way street: try to figure out what you can do for your potential mentor. It may be small gestures, but it shows you value their time and are not just concerned with yourself.

Use accountability groups. Facebook groups are popular these days for online communities, but there are also now specific groups that exist for accountability. In fact, while writing this book I joined a couple of Facebook groups for authors: *SassyZenGirl Networking Group*:

https://www.facebook.com/groups/SassyZenGirl/

and *Self-Publishing Made Simple:*

https://www.facebook.com/groups/selfpubmadesimple

Set a hard deadline. If you have, or can arrange, a hard deadline, this is a powerful accountability motivator. For example, if you have fitness goals, even if they're not exactly related, you can sign up for an upcoming Spartan Run, 5K, Fun Run or whatever is appropriate to your expected level of fitness. Whatever your field or passion is, you can probably find other events to give you a hard deadline. Because the deadline is non-negotiable you're either all-in or not and will find ways to instead negotiate with yourself to get the work done.

If you don't have a hard deadline, then you can make a firm one by publicly declaring your project and deadline. I am not necessarily a proponent for oversharing your personal projects and goals because it invites all kinds of unsolicited and "helpful" feedback you don't need in your life. However, once you have done the groundwork and are satisfied yourself with your plan, to go ahead and announce your goal and target to the world is a great motivator because then you'll want to avoid the embarrassment and public humiliation of failing to make your deadline. Ok, it's probably not all that bad, but it's surprising how it can self-motivate you to make that goal when someone is potentially watching and waiting.

***

Use an accountability app. My last option--and maybe the most fun one--is to *use an app to hold yourself accountable.* Yes, there's an app for that--several of them, actually.

One such app is stickK, at:
https://www.stickk.com

StickK works by having you sign up for a "Commitment Contract" which is a binding agreement you sign with *yourself* to leverage the power of loss aversion and accountability to drive you to complete your goal. According to the stickK website:

"By asking our users to sign Commitment Contracts, stickK helps users define their goal (whatever it may be), acknowledge what it'll take to accomplish it, and leverage the power of putting money on the line to turn that goal into a reality."

Wait, what? Money on the line? That's right--when creating your Commitment Contract, you can decide how much money (optional) you will put on the line and who will receive the money (a charitable organization) if you are unable to keep your commitment. How's that for a motivator? It may sound a little complicated and scary (it's supposed be a little bit scary) but it's a straightforward process, and you have the stickK community to help you and cheer you on. The process is:

1. Define a goal
2. Put a stake (money) on the line (if you want)
3. Invite a Referee
4. Invite Supporters

After signing up for your Commitment Contract, you

proceed and work on your goal and submit a *report* when you've successfully completed the work. Supporters can see your progress, and if you elect a referee she or he will keep you honest. If you fail to turn in a success report, you will forfeit your stake (money). If you're up for the challenge, it's a pretty cool way to light a fire under your butt, put your money where your mouth is, and get your thing done.

There are other accountability apps out there such as Beeminder (https://www.beeminder.com). You should do a Google search to find the latest since some apps come and go by nature.

Summary:
You absolutely want to establish some concrete mechanism for accountability for your projects and goals.

Coach For Accountability?

You can teach yourself a lot of knowledge and skills on your own. I am a big fan of self-learning. You can survey the landscape across a number of experts, or so-called experts and make your own decisions about what is BS and what is not. You can learn at your own pace. You can learn what you want to learn at that moment, which is one of the best ways to learn.

Given all that, and since this is meant to be a complete self-improvement book and system, I'm not going to go into great detail on this next topic, but I will touch on the option for enlisting a *coach* for accountability. Why might you do that?

There are 2 things that self-learning will not give you.

1. Experience

You can't get experience from a book. Sure you can learn tips about what not to do, and this helps. But no amount of reading or training videos will give you experience on having a baby. Nor can it give you experience on running a business.

Because you don't know what you don't know.
Because you don't know how you will react emotionally until you are immersed in the experience.

2. External accountability

If you are reading or listening to this, chances are you are a responsible person who is accountable to any number of people or things. You are accountable to a job. You are accountable to your family. You may be accountable to your church or other organization.

I have been there. I am still there. There are times I felt the crushing weight of everyone's expectations and felt stuck with no way to move. Even if I had any energy left, I had no time to make any significant change. Now some of the principles and techniques I am teaching you will help you eliminate some of this burden and effectively find the time.

But that still leaves a problem with accountability. Because if you are accountable to something or someone, you will try to be accountable, and meet those expectations. This goes back to the *Urgent vs. Important* principle. Making transformational change in your life may be important to you, but it is not urgent compared to the things you are accountable for. You can try to be accountable to yourself, but it's really hard. When push comes to shove--and it does pretty much every day--you will tend to be accountable to everyone but yourself.

One answer to both problems is coaching. An appropriate coach will work outside of yourself to provide guidance based on objective observation and experience. A coach will give you the accountability you need to succeed.

So how do you know coaching will make a difference? Well, by coaching I am talking in the broader consulting sense, but to answer the question, there is no better place to look than the case of an athletic coach because we have all seen it in practice in sports. Do you think any Olympic competitor could ever get even close to a medal without a coach?

Every professional football team or other sports team is filled with professional, experienced athletes. Yet, can you imagine a team playing even one professional game without a coach? They'd be lost, or at the very least dysfunctional. An athlete—whether solo or team player—is too inside their own head to coach themselves. It's no different for business, life or transformational change.

By being accountable to someone else: the coach, you have now moved the accountability outside of yourself, and to someone who wants you to succeed. Someone to whom you are responsible for showing regular progress to. Now, you can prioritize your personal transformation and make it as urgent as your other responsibilities.

Now you may be thinking: well, I'll just be accountable to my spouse, friend, co-worker or family member. Most likely not. None of those people are interested in you succeeding. And worse, they have a whole spectrum of reasons to want you to fail and to maintain the status quo, because of how it affects them personally or emotionally.

By enlisting a coach:

- You are working with someone who genuinely wants you to succeed.
- You introduced real accountability to your efforts.
- You have a coach with visibility outside of your own head.
- Your chances of success may go up significantly.

Accountability is liberating, because accountability means success. You may have heard other motivational speakers say to "Give yourself permission to succeed." That's great, but as you should know by now, I am all about actionable advice versus vague inspirational quotes. Accountability, which comes from a trusted coach, does not give you permission to succeed but instead gives you "A mission to succeed."

Permission To Succeed vs. Mission To Succeed

Inspiration gives you permission to succeed. Which means it *may* happen, but rarely does once the emotion wears off. Coaching and accountability give you a mission —an actual plan and timeframe. This is why coaching and mentorship work, and is the secret of many successful people. Even people who are already successful, and you could argue already have all the skills they could need, are leveraging the value of coaching to provide the accountability and the empowerment to achieve. I was surprised to learn how many people in the top of their fields actively enlist coaching. Coaching is one of the best ways for rapid actual change as well as to stay competitive and keep growing.

Here is another important point about coaching: trading dollars for time and results. This was a revelation to me. I was always so obsessed with doing everything myself in order to save money. Maybe this is you too, and it's not a bad thing. For one thing, until you start meeting your success goals, you don't have much money. Also in business it makes sense to watch your spending. The problem is: to make transformational change, you always need to make some kind of investment. I thought that investing my time was the only way. But I learned that really successful people know how to trade money for rapid change. There is a saying that goes: "If you can use money to make a problem go away, then it is not a problem."

Now of course you should always make intelligent decisions about spending your money. But most of us err largely on the side of saving money at all costs, and this can be self-defeating.

I know a lot of people who spend large sums of money on gear, equipment or capital. Things which start depreciating immediately. Yet they will not make an investment in personal change that will last them a lifetime. Coaching comes at a price, and quality coaching comes at a quality price. However, the payback can be accelerated and many-fold.

So in conclusion, should you get a coach? It really depends on you. You can get all the accountability you need by using previously discussed options like mentors, and tribes such as Facebook groups. Also, coaching engagements can become their own distraction depending on the motives of the coach. And finally, I'm wired to be self-starting, and in my experience, there are good reasons to maintain control and to *delegate* versus handing over too much control to someone else. However, I realize that other people are wired differently and may really need solid external accountability. If so, go for it. Just be sure *you* control the goals and targets.

The 5 Second Rule

Whatever your passion is, whatever your project is, whatever you feel a burning need to do, start it now. *Right now*.

To overcome friction, it's very important to teach yourself how to get out of your own head and "just do it," Nike style. Whenever I did this, things somehow always seems to work out better. Whenever I didn't, I ended up regretting it. But over time I trained myself to internalize this principle and get much better at initializing a new project or task reflexively without thinking.

The problem is, if you're like most of us, your mind will instantly come up with a variety of reasons exactly why you can't start now. In fact, you might agree that sometimes we spend more time thinking about why we can't do something than it would have taken just to go ahead and do it. Here are some of the reasons your clever-but-procrastinating brain might come up with for not starting, and my answers to them:

Your brain: "I need more information."
My answer: No you don't. Outline something based on what you already know. Then once you have something down on paper you can come back and keep refining it later.

Your brain: "No really, I have no idea what I'm talking about."
My answer: Great! Write something anyway. You already have a passion for the topic, yes, or you wouldn't be here? Write down what you are passionate about. Write

the reasons why you want or need to do this, like you're talking to your diary. Let this stream of consciousness come out and see where it leads.

Your brain: "I can't. I'm really busy."
My answer: Then jot down something—anything—and build on it here and there, whenever you have some minutes:
- Make some bullet point tasks. Write down your questions.
- Preferably: make a rough sketch diagram of your project.
- Draw a quick mind map; this works for about anything: from answering questions, to task lists, to areas of exploration.

Your brain: "It sounds good, but I'm really having trouble getting started."
My answer: Use the "5 Second Rule".

Um, use the *what* rule?

Mel Robbins is the author of *The 5 Second Rule: Transform your Life, Work, and Confidence with Everyday Courage*,[1] a motivational book that is all about reducing friction and enabling you to make decisions and take actions to change and improve your life. She refers to these as "daily acts of courage."

According to Robbins's research, when we have an idea, impulse or decision, we have only 5 seconds to act on that. If we wait any longer than that, all the emotions and self-doubt start to creep in. And subsequently, we start making the excuses and rationalizations for our inaction. The result is we never take action, *especially* if that action takes us out of our comfort zone.

Based on that, Robbins' simple but effective solution is: whenever you first get an impulse or urge to take a new step, try something new, approach someone new, or start a difficult or scary task you *must* count backward from 5 to 1 and *act immediately*:

5, 4, 3, 2, 1, GO!

It's like Nike's "Just Do It" slogan on steroids. The problem with advice like that (Just do it) is that it fails to answer the question: "But how?" The 5 Second Rule provides a simple but powerful mechanism to at least get started doing something. Robbins' book goes into detail about how she conceived and developed this method at a low point in her life and how it turned her life around as well as the lives of others since then.

It seems like an overly simple method, but since Robbins first revealed the idea on a TEDx stage, it has become one of the top 20 TEDx talks in the world and has been viewed almost 14 million times in over 37 countries[2].

So apparently she is not alone (nor you, nor I)--a lot of people have trouble getting past that first friction or inertia and getting the ball rolling. And that's often the toughest part. Probably you've experienced that yourself: the "writer's block," the staring at a blank computer screen but if you somehow get started you often get in the zone and the creative thoughts start flowing.

The hard part is just getting started, trying to get yourself up off that couch when you know you should be cranking out some work, but it feels so comfortable right now and--by golly--those cat videos on social media are not going to "like" themselves.

There's nothing wrong with you--you're just human and get tired, both emotionally and physically, and have all kinds of thoughts and emotions to process. But as the previous numbers show, you're not alone so don't beat yourself up. Use the simple 5 Second Rule to get out of your head quickly and get the "flow" state started.

* * *

Summary:
Use the simple but powerful 5 Second Rule to eliminate friction and get started right now on your next One thing.

Start With The Acorn

Ok, I talked about starting *right now*. By the way, if you did that and are no longer reading this book, I'm ok with that and consider it a win. I'll wait here until you come back...

Welcome back. And now let's elaborate a bit on how you can get started in a frictionless way.

Let's say you have an idea or a new passion, but you really don't have much knowledge on the subject or know where to start. One thing you can do, then, is to start outlining what you don't know by getting all your questions, concerns and even fears down on paper. Every question you have is a concrete action item you can execute to find an answer. Every fear you have is a mini research task to search the web and find out how other people dealt with that fear.

It's true you don't know what you don't know. However, this process will let you use your creative powers to try and imagine and visualize the aspects of the project, good and bad. Even if you find out later you were way off in your guesses, you will still internalize and retain that knowledge much better than if you were to read about the subject matter passively. Learning a new subject area or process--or just about anything really--is more effective when you focus on the gaps and questions in your own mind, and not the flow of learning outlined by a textbook or someone else.

This could be the subject of an entire book or research career, but to summarize, you should start with whatever mental seed you have. Let's call that idea seed your acorn.

Your task, then, is to start with that acorn (your idea) and start growing that into a mighty oak tree (your accomplished body of work), nurturing it (your expertise) along the way. If you start by trying to figure out an entire oak tree you will just get overwhelmed trying to learn and create all the branches at once.

Even worse is if you try to compare your small oak sapling with someone else's oak tree. That can be counterproductive as well as depressing because you will get de-motivated. You need to remember you are in a different part of your growth than they are. You can't easily see all the hard work and time that went into getting where they are. Further, in any journey of accomplishment, there are going to be things that come easier for you, and things that come harder. That person you are negatively comparing yourself to is almost certainly struggling in some other area you don't see.

Finally, don't get discouraged if you are in an early phase of your growth and feel like others are way ahead because:

- If you use the Less Is More mindset and tactics you can fast-track major chunks of your time.
- You want to follow your *own* growth, not someone else's. You should employ bits of your own experience you already have to not only create your own unique results but also leverage expertise, aspects, and style you already honed to help shortcut the process.

Summary:
- Start with the acorn, not the tree.
- Use your own unique and existing experience and style like a super formula to accelerate your work and growth.

Be A Time Squirrel

Let me extend the acorn analogy a bit further. There are basically two ways to find time to work on your neglected core art:

1. Block out larger time chunks similar to Keller's ONE Thing system
2. Grab small chunklets of time wherever you can.

Larger chunks are better from a Less Is More mindset because 1) you can focus and 2) the goal is to reduce the hectic switching back and forth between tasks.

But I recognize that for some/many people chunklets may be the way to go or at least a way to start building your Less Is More mindset. Also, it may be effective to block larger chunks of time on certain mornings and then use the chunklet approach to augment the major chunks.

Use the chunklets approach like a squirrel, actively gathering acorns when and where she finds them. Similarly, you can opportunistically grab chunklets of productivity between other tasks, or when you're waiting on something (which seems to happen quite often, even for busy people). By itself, one acorn is not much, but over time the squirrel has a nice big stockpile built up. Likewise, if you are writing a book or blog pieces or whatever, writing a chunklet at a time will help you build a nice stockpile of content.

This will require some discipline on your part; committing to a simple system for efficiently capturing the chunklets as you go. I use Evernote as my tool to capture ideas and content but there are other tools that can do the same job so use whatever works for you as long as you can easily (frictionlessly) open it and capture your thoughts. And you don't have to use a digital tool (for capture), you can go analog with pen and paper as I discuss elsewhere in this book.

If writing in an old school journal works for you then use that. It may seem like extra work to later transcribe this into digital form but keep in mind that the hard part is usually composing the content in the first place. Transcribing it into a digital tool is straightforward and doesn't require creativity or a lot of energy.

Even though the chunklet approach is less in line with the Less Is More mindset in terms of removing the complexity of life, I think it's important to consider because it still lets you get more of your core art done which reduces your stress level overall and increases your sense of accomplishment. And again you can mix both large time chunks and chunklet approaches. I still advocate using both more in the morning when you have more energy.

Some advantages of the chunklet approach include:

Capturing a thought when productivity strikes. You can always just capture the skeleton of the idea, so you don't forget it, and flesh it out later. That way you don't risk losing the idea because you waited until your next focus time chunk session. If you're like me you know it's frustrating to have a great idea or thought and then lose it.

Another advantage is it helps minimize those mental interrupts. If you try to hold in your mind all those little things you "can't forget to do later" they will be a distraction from getting other work done. Capture the thought and then let it go from your mind.

168 Hours

"Effective people outsource, ignore or minimize everything else."
Laura Vanderkam

Laura Vanderkam is another author/speaker whose philosophy agrees with the Less Is More philosophy (Not surprising, or I probably wouldn't mention her, right?). According to Vanderkam:

"I've found that these people focus, as much as possible, on what I call their core competencies...Effective people outsource, ignore or minimize everything else."

What she calls "core competencies" resonates with my idea of "core art" and for our purposes is essentially the same. As I have said, I prefer "art" because it sounds more like a passion. Also, you may not be competent in your art in the beginning, but these principles still apply.

Vanderkam has further made great contributions in the area of productivity by extensively studying and coaching people on how they spend their time.

Her basic conclusion (backed by data) is: you have more time than you think.

In fact, she wrote the book on it entitled: *168 Hours: You Have More Time Than You Think*[1]. To prove this, she advises you on how to create a "time log" and document how you are *actually* spending your time every day—not how you *think* you are spending your when asked off the top of your head. Using time logs she has, for example, proven that workers frequently overestimate how many hours they work per week on their actual job. Your mileage may vary, but this turns out to be the case whether you are an office worker, entrepreneur or business owner. This is not to say you aren't busy, but it serves as a basis to understand how you are really spending your time. By using a time log—and using it honestly—you will have the data you need to help you make real changes.

The time log shows if you're spending time on your core competencies/art. It also shows where your priorities are. According to Vanderkam, you chose where to spend your time so whatever you chose to spend the *most* time on is probably where your priorities are. This is not to say you aren't driven by other forces that aren't your core art, such as taking care of children or not wanting to get fired and lose your income. But by recognizing your motivations for the priorities you place on your time you can start to consciously realign them to improve how you *spend* your time. By doing so, you can find how to eliminate time wasters and reclaim more time for your core art.

Many of the systems and tactics I discuss in this book involve *subtracting* things--things like distractions and too many priorities. This makes sense with a Less Is More mindset.

Because, like me, you may be skeptical about the idea that you can squeeze a few more hours into your already exhausting week. Well, you're not alone. Most of the advice you read for getting more done in your day or week involves finding scraps of time you can steal back to get more work done. However, I felt like the same tired and trivial tips I kept reading would only result in minimal gains. I wanted more than scraps of time. I was looking for something with more of a payoff. I wanted to take it to the next level.

No technique is going to change the laws of time and physics and add more hours into a week. Everybody gets the same number of hours: 168 to be exact. But how you approach and use those 168 hours make all the difference.

This is where Vanderkam's approach shines. She turns the idea of subtraction on its head, and instead she advocates starting with a clean slate of the 168 hours you or I get in any given week. And in doing so she quite thoroughly and convincingly argues that this is a lot of time. This is how it works:

- Start with 168 hours.
- Now subtract the actual hours you work on your main job. The actual hours as based on your time long, not an inflated estimate. Let's say it was 50 realistic hour. 168 - 50 = 118 hours
- Now start subtracting life necessities. Let's allow a generous 8hrs per night of sleep. That's 56 hours per week, so 118 - 56 = 62 hours
- Subtract 2 hours per day for eating. 62 - 14 = 48
- Some time for hygiene is good too (for all of us, thank you). An hour per day: 48 - 7 = 41.
- Let's subtract 2 hours per day for relationships. You can argue that you are the kind of person that spends much more time with your family or whoever per day. But do you really spend quality time or do you spend hours watching TV and don't really spend time in a way that improves the quality of your relationships? I am not judging—we all do it, but this is a choice and an opportunity for improvement. So, 41 - 14 = 27
- You have 27 hours left over in the week!

That leaves *almost 4 hours per day* left over you could use on your core art! Yes, I know you will argue that you do other things like commuting, child care, and cleaning. But my point, and Vanderkam's, is: you have a lot of time in your week, even after you subtract time for all the things above. And even if you are a busy person or take care of children, you still have hours left over, and those are all negotiable.

Some other notes

You may be thinking I'm a guy and I don't know what it's like to be a mother. Well, this is the 21st Century, and I did my share of our children's care including diapers, feedings, bath time, and rides and walks to school. I also split housework with my wife and have done much of the cooking and dishes for many years. I'm not saying it's easy —in fact I know from experience it's not, but it's doable, and more doable if you employ Less Is More principles. In fact, I urge you to do this, instead of trying to burn the candle at both ends. Because what you will be burning, is burning yourself out.

Life is too short to spend all day or weekend cleaning. Do enough and move on. Outsource it or get a better system. Vanderkam, in her *168 Hours* book, goes into a lot of detail on your options for housekeeping so if you are interested to know more in that regard then check out her writing.

You don't need hours of nonproductive day job time. Instead, you need to make your day job hours productive. You can use many of the same principles in this book to do that. At the end of the day, results count. By working long hours repeatedly in an attempt to be a martyr and impress your management gives diminishing returns. Instead, get them used to your work-life balance and working reasonable hours, and save working after hours for when it really counts. Generally they will respect you more for this. If not, then you need to reconsider the terms of your position or look for other opportunities.

You aren't obligated for hours of mindless family or social time where you don't even connect. Spend the right kind of time and defend the rest for yourself. Schedule time with your spouse or significant other. Specify a rough time, even if it's just for watching TV, and be present when you spend that time and don't multitask. This allows you to get core art done while you have more energy and then spend some chill time. Also, once you are successful at establishing your core time early in the day, you won't be working on it much at night.

Also make rough, but concrete plans, ahead of the weekend. If plans were made for you, then use that. Hey since we're going to x, then I am going to work on y at z time.

If you do the most productive work for your job, and spend meaningful time with spouse and family, then you're cheating no-one. So stop cheating yourself.

Summary:
You have a lot of hours (168) in your week.
Start with a clean slate and see how much is left over.
Now, what are you doing with those other hours? Exactly. Put them to good use.

Go Analog

    I felt compelled to add this chapter on going analog (versus digital) for a couple of reasons. One is that we are finding ourselves ever more caught up in an always-on digital world. When we aren't spending our time at work hunched over a computer, we are staring down at our phones for hours. Although this makes for some funny clips on YouTube where someone, engrossed in their phone, walks into a water fountain, it's a terrible trend for our postures, relationships, and quality of life.

    Which leads me into my second reason: that analog is just better--in terms of being a richer experience. Texting someone is a huge step backwards in terms of sensory experience. That's why we have to use emojis to explain our mood which would be very obvious if we were talking to someone in person. And it's not just a visual thing--the overall experience in person is better because more of the senses are involved. That creates a better experience and better quality, longer-lasting memories. Digital is a lower fidelity experience. Also it's hard to defend when you're physically present with other people, but you're not mentally present; you're engrossed in your phone instead of being truly present with them.

    I'm not a technophobe or Luddite. I am educated in, work with, and use technology constantly. The reason texting and social media are so popular is that they let us connect with other people, places, and information that we would otherwise be unable to experience. But again, it is a step backward in terms of richness of experience and its negative impact on in-person experiences.

    But still, why am I talking about analog in a

productivity book? The reason is that analog activities enhance our creative process more than digital, and that leads to a more productive and enjoyable daily experience. And I am not the only person to assert this[1].

- The process of putting pen to paper in a journal
- Writing out song lyrics by hand
- Drawing a mind map
- Brainstorming thoughts on sticky notes and putting them up
- Writing on a whiteboard, or with chalk on an old school chalkboard even.

So don't give up your digital lifestyle, but throw in some analog activities. If the idea of journaling appeals to you, go ahead and do that. The creative boost you get will spill over into your other work.

When you are brainstorming, researching, or designing, consider doing your original work with a pen or pencil in a composition book or sketchbook. You can always quickly transfer them to digital form later. The key difference is you won't be distracted by the tool while you are exercising your creative muscles.

Use mind maps for—well a variety of things actually. You can use them for initial brainstorming, for memorization or for doing some analysis when you get stuck on a problem. I know there are apps to let you create mind maps, but they just don't work for my right brain in the same way that a pen and a notebook does.

If you are learning a new skill, write facts or notes on colorful stickies and place them on your mirror, on your door, wall, fridge—wherever. I put them on my guitar sometimes.

In fact, put stickies wherever inspiration guides you. Put them on things in your house to label them if you are learning a new language. Put them on your bathroom mirror to inspire you in the morning. Put them on your refrigerator to keep you on track.

In the next chapter, I will discuss a system to use sticky notes for simple task management.

Summary:
Embrace some old-school analog methods.

The 3 Column Sticky System

"Sticky notes" or "stickies" are proof that analog works, even in a modern digital world. For anyone reading this who has not worked in an office since the 1990s or maybe lived in an isolated monastery in Tibet* and don't know what they are, a sticky note is a slip of notepaper having an adhesive strip on the back that allows them to be attached to, and removal from, a surface without leaving any sticky residue. If you're curious about the history of sticky notes, which were invented by 3M and officially branded as Post-It Notes, you can go to this Wikipedia entry:

https://en.wikipedia.org/wiki/Post-it_Note

Sticky notes are used for many applications in the business world such as taking phone messages, writing little reminders to oneself, and violating corporate security policy by visibly posting passwords near your computer for all to see. Sticky notes originally came in a particular shade of yellow but have since been sold in a variety of colors.

The reason for the popularity of sticky notes is because of the particular adhesive they contain which doesn't stick really well. Normally that would be a terrible feature for glue, but it turned out to be a great feature for little paper notes because they can be easily removed and moved without leaving a sticky mess or harming the surface they are stuck to.

This movable nature of the sticky notes is what makes them perfect for the 3 column tasking system I'm about to describe (yes, I'm finally getting to the point of this chapter). Sticky notes have been used in a variety of productivity systems including the *Design Thinking* process developed at Stanford and in the *Agile Scrum* process for software development.

Aside from their convenient sticky properties, the notes are fast and convenient to write and therefore don't hamper the creative process. They also engage multiple senses. And finally, they promote an effective collaborative environment for teams who can write, share, and see each other's notes.

You could Google to research ways to use sticky notes for productivity. But I am going to give you a simple, generic system you can use for task management, which I will call the "3 Column Sticky System." As the name implies, this systems consists of some kind of board (or wall) with 3 columns, those columns being:

TO DO, DOING, DONE

The exact wall surface is not important as long as the sticky notes actually stick to it--usually a flat, smooth surface. I use the back of a door in my home office. A refrigerator will work too as long as no-one messes with your notes. A standard office dry-erase whiteboard is perfect because you can write the column names with the dry-erase markers, and also draw vertical lines if you want.

Here is a picture of what a 3 Column Sticky Board looks like:

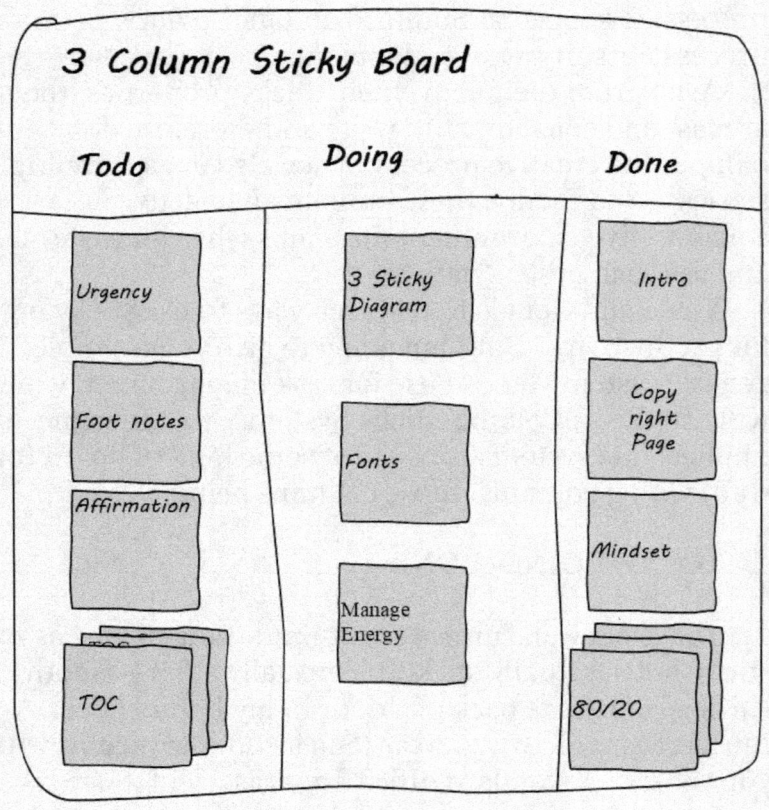

It's really that simple and the columns are self-explanatory. You write out tasks on the sticky notes and post them starting in the TO DO column.

Then when you start to work on a task, you move that sticky note to the DOING column, and when you are finished with the task you move it to the done column.

The system seems overly simple and that's exactly why I am recommending it. I have used this same approach for highly technical development projects. And I have used a variety of team-based collaboration software tools and it's still hard to beat this one, especially for personal productivity. I am using it to write this book, so I am "eating my own dog food," as they say.

It may seem like you can just do this in your head, or with a digital to-do list. Maybe you can, but after observing and using this in a variety of situations, for most people this just works better:

- The multi-sensory experience is there: the visual colors, the feel of the paper, and maybe even the smell of the marker.
- The visual reminder aspect of the board: a physical board, especially with vibrant colors is harder to ignore and is a great motivator. Whereas a digital tool can be out of sight and out of mind on your laptop.
- There is a certain sense of accomplishment and a mini rush you get when knocking off and physically moving notes (and therefore tasks). You don't get the same experience in a software tool.
- It's fast and easy, and therefore low-friction. My handwriting is terrible, and I don't use it much, but still the sticky note process feels faster and easier.

Time Frame

Your choice of time frame for the board is a personal preference, and you may want to experiment with what works best for you. The time frame you use dictates the amount of work you load into the TO-DO column. Time frames could be daily, weekly, 2-week sprints, 21 days, or continuous. Certain systems like "Agile Scrum" operate on a time boxing principle and strongly enforce a regular cycle of work, for example, 2 weeks. In other words, you load just enough work into your TODO column that you expect to be able to do in 2 weeks (or whatever your period), and then proceed to work on only those tasks for the period. The key principle of time boxing is that you strongly resist adding new tasks which disrupt your existing work and cause you to miss your deadline. Instead you only (or mostly) work on those set of tasks, try to get them all done in the defined period, and then clear your board at the end of the period and repeat the process.

Other approaches just have you adding tasks continuously into the "queue" which steadily get worked and move to the DONE column. If you are using this for a particular project or deliverable, I would suggest you don't take the continuous approach as it allows more and more work to creep in (known as "scope creep") which can cause your completion date to keep slipping and slipping.

In any case, I strongly recommend you use the board on a daily basis. This means you must get good at breaking down your work into one or more tasks that can be completed in a single day. This is the best way to keep the system going because you will get to feel the process every day and internalize it as a good habit.

Other tips

Use different colored sticky notes to represent different types of tasks. They could represent different categories within a project, or represent your different goal areas like business, fitness, or self-development. Don't obsess over this--just use the colors to keep it fun and interesting.

Let tasks stack up like messy leaves in the DONE column so they show just how much you're getting done.

At the end of your chosen time frame (for example one week), reset the board, Clean off the DONE stickies and load the TO DO column with your new set of tasks.

Summary:

Use the 3 Column Sticky system as a simple way to manage your tasks like a boss.

*Actually, I'll bet those Tibetan Monks, with their vows of silence, use sticky notes like nobody's business.

The Minimum Viable Product

One of the biggest challenges of completing a project is, well, actually completing it. One of the obstacles to completion is perfectionism, where you want to keep reworking something or thinking you can make it just a little bit better. I've been guilty of it myself: "I can make this website prettier if I just do this...". "I'm unhappy with this song. I need to add more cowbell...". The reality is that your work is probably never going to be perfect, so you have to learn to let it go at some point. It usually helps to make a clear list of "acceptance criteria," in other words, what would constitute an acceptable completion of your project. You need to do this up front, not in the middle of, or late in the project. When you meet this list, you have a project that's good enough to release to the world, because you *agree with yourself*, based on your acceptance criteria.

Another problem with completing a project is simply trying to do too much. In the world of software development there is a concept of the "Minimum Viable Product" or "MVP." In software development and especially on the Web it is crucial to get something out there quickly. It may be counterintuitive sometimes but getting a crude app launched sooner is strategically better than waiting to release a full-featured version of the product. To define the Minimum Viable Product, you have to make some hard decisions and aggressively start slashing some of those features of your work or product. You have to ask: what is the real minimum functionality which will allow the user to do what they need to do?

In their book *Rework*[1,] Jason Fried and David Heinemeier Hansson cover in great detail how streamlining your app or product has positive and strategic benefits. You can always add features later, but the important thing is to get your work in the hands of your users or customers. Further, they make the strong case that you should never add too many features or options in a product.

The idea of a Minimum Viable Product does not just apply to software; you can use the principle to guide any kind of project. Are you trying to be too ambitious in that event you are planning? Are there too many buttons on that new blender you are designing? Would something more minimalistic or elegant work just as well or better? Are you trying to add too many tracks and instruments to that song--would something more raw be good? Have you outlined fitness goals worthy of an Ironman (and risking failure to meet them) when all you really need to be shooting for is a 5K obstacle run? In these examples and others, you can get a sense that not only can you get away with doing less, but the result might also actually be better. In other words, at the risk of repeating myself: Less Is More.

Summary:
Leverage the Minimum Viable Product principle to reduce the work needed to complete your project.

Manage Energy, Not Time

Let me describe to you how I used to try and get my core art projects done. See if it sounds familiar to you. I would get up with just enough time to do my morning shower, complete the rest of my get-ready-for-work ritual, and commute to work. Then I would spend an intellectually draining—and sometimes emotionally draining (dealing with people)—full day on my day job. Then I would do the commute back home and make, eat and clean up after dinner. If I timed it right I could squeeze in a workout while something was cooking. Next, I would spend some time with my wife or kids watching TV. Finally, when all that is done and the kids are in bed, it's like 10 pm at night. So I'm really going to open my laptop, or go to my little home studio, and try to work on my core art project? How could I possibly expect to have any energy left to do anything? I didn't.

Let me clarify one thing: this did not just happen with my passion-related core art projects or goals. This was true whether or not my core art project was personal *or* for a work-related project. Before I started learning and applying Less Is More principles, I would spend my entire work day attending meetings and getting urgent-but-not-important tasks done. That meant if I wanted to make any progress on my strategic work projects I had to work on them at night when not only was my energy low, but I should have been spending it on other priorities like family and self-improvement.

In the subtitle of their bestseller book *The Power of Full Engagement*[1], authors Jim Loehr (performance psychologist and co-founder of the Human Performance

Institute), and Tony Schwartz (author and CEO of The Energy Project) evangelize their principle that:

"Managing Energy, Not Time, Is the Key to High Performance and Personal Renewal."

Put another way, in order to be a consistently high performer; you have to focus on *managing your energy, not your time*[2]. Most of us are familiar with the times when we seem to get in the zone and are just cranking out the work or content, which makes us feel good about ourselves (and should). We've also been advised for a long to time to get our thoughts down "when inspiration strikes." The problem is we don't want to depend on the randomness of experiencing those moments. The reality underlying those bursts of creativity is that they tend to happen when we are relaxed and full of energy.

I'm not going to tell you, like everyone else, to get plenty of sleep because we can do better than that. Instead, I'm going to give you this nifty diagram of what your energy looks like during the day:

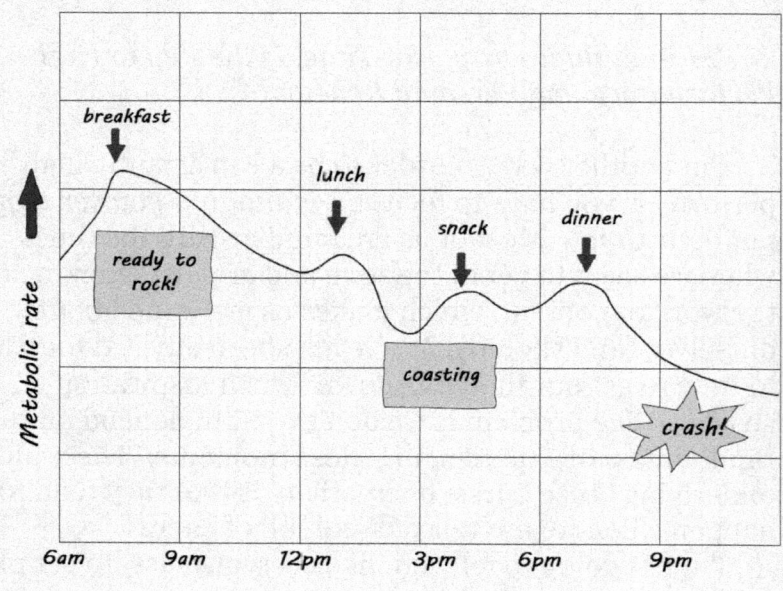

We are creatures of biology, and it's hard to escape the fact that we will only perform well for so long before we need to rest or recharge. Sure you extend that time using stimulants like coffee or by sheer determination, but sooner or later you're going to crash[1].

As the graph in the diagram shows, your energy is going to be the highest after you've slept. It will drop slowly over the day in general and have peaks and valleys during that time.

The things that increase your energy are:

- Sleep
- Eating
- Taking a break
- Experiencing a positive emotional event

None of those things should be earth-shattering revelations but--having said that--do you (or most people) consciously plan around them? Many people:

- Coast in the morning and try to catch up at the end of the day
- Eat infrequent, large meals
- Work for long periods at a mediocre pace, without taking a break
- Let ourselves be surrounded by negative people and environments.

So even though our sources of energy are fairly obvious, we are rudely ignoring them. In the context of managing your energy, all of a sudden those overused gems of advice start to make sense:

- Do your most important work in the morning before

urgent or menial tasks like checking email.
- Eat more, smaller meals throughout the day.
- Limit your blocks of work time and take breaks.
- Surround yourself with positive people and a positive environment.

I don't believe you need to go hardcore doing all these things, but ignoring all of them is a recipe for mediocrity. First and foremost, I would figure out some way you can work on your important core art in the morning (or if you work a different shift: whenever you wake up) when you are most rested. This will probably have the most impact. I would also work actively on surrounding yourself with positivity because that will make everything better.

If you can do these two things the others will tend to work themselves out. Also, you may find them harder to execute if you don't control all your time during the day. My advice is to front-load your important core art early in your day, and having achieved that, you can deal with the important-but-not-urgent stuff in the 2nd half when energy matters less, and you won't stress about it because you already *won the day*.

Summary:
Focus on working with your energy, not your time.
Prioritize you core art early in the day
Proactively work on maintaining a positive environment

LESS Barriers Actions

1. Accountability is key. Establish concrete accountability checks for your projects.
2. Use the Hemingway Method to reduce friction.
3. Start with the acorn.
4. Use the 5 Second Rule to remove inertia and "start now."
5. Study and wisely use your 168 hours.
6. Consider adopting some analog methods like The 3 Column Sticky System.
7. Leverage the Minimum Viable Product principle to start finishing.
8. Focus on working with your energy, not your time.

MORE Done

The Enjoy-Matters Matrix

In my research I wanted a way to somehow capture with an image what is at the root of the discontent and quiet desperation that many of us feel at one time or another. Toward that, I developed my own matrix, the "Enjoy-Matters Matrix" which looks like this:

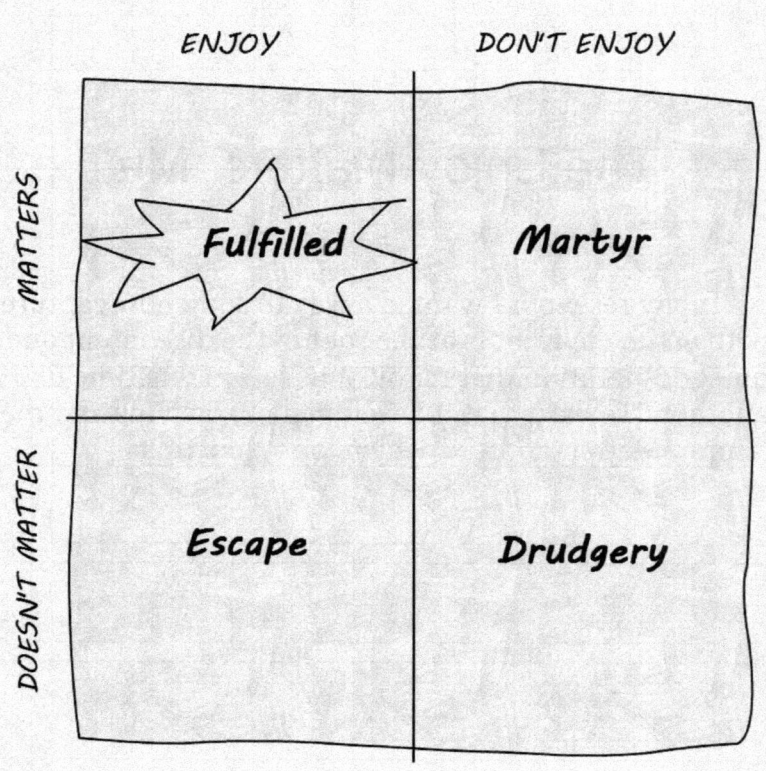

You've may have heard the quote:
"Choose a job you love, and you will never have to work a day in your life."

I know that quote is meant to be inspirational but honestly I think it's a little glib and possibly even deceptively harmful.

Glib because it's misleading and discounts all the hard work that goes into any career or pursuit, even if you're totally passionate about it. Whether or not you believe it takes *10,000 hours*[1] to be great at something, any lasting achievement will take a lot of hard work. Harmful, because it can have the unintended consequence of making someone think that if they are *NOT* loving their job every single day, then they are doing their life all wrong and it will cause them to be depressed.

So I won't be a Pollyanna about this. For the record, I'm not a person who uses quaint or old-fashioned sounding words, but I like that one. If you're not familiar with the term, a Pollyanna is:

"an excessively or blindly optimistic person."

Now, I don't mean to criticize anyone who is optimistic by nature and in truth you should surround yourself with those kind of people. But on the other hand, you might know that person who always tries to tell you how much they love their job and always tries to tell you your glass is half full, no matter what happens to you. Yes, you may get an even better job after you were laid off. Yes, if you survive cancer, you might feel blessed with every new day. But let's be honest, if you got laid off or just got diagnosed with cancer, your glass is not half full. Your life sucks right now. And pretending everything is great is not helpful to you. But even if you don't have such a dramatic, life-changing situation that doesn't mean you don't have a problem or don't have a right to feel unhappy or discontent. If day after day you don't enjoy the job you are doing right now it's not a blessing, and it's something you want to think about changing in some way.

Having said all that, I do agree it's important to enjoy the work you generally do. But I can't imagine any job, no matter how glamorous it looks on the surface, that doesn't have boring or unpleasant tasks that go along with it.

What Matters

Putting the focus external to yourself has benefits to you as well.

It can really help you maintain a focus and serve as a personal compass when you feel lost or confused about where to go next.

"Matters" means it has to matter to you. Your work has to matter to you, to who you are and your own situation which is different from everyone else's. If what matters to you is having a good time, then you should do that and you probably don't need any advice from me. I won't even judge you (ok, secretly I am). But chances are if you're reading this book, you have occasionally or frequently questioned if you what you are doing matters. You may wonder if what you are doing has any meaning and if not are you wasting your life?

The problem is that on a daily basis you usually don't have or make any breakthroughs. Your success usually comes from completing a series of small tasks or making small wins. When you spend your day working on tasks that feel trivial or non-life-changing--and do this day after day--it's easy to start feeling like you're going nowhere with your life.

Alternately, you may question if you are making a difference in anyone else's life. Some people like nurses and first responders have jobs where they can directly see the impact they make on others' lives. Many of us are not as lucky if we work in the retail or business world.

Let me share a story about a friend and co-worker from years ago when we were developing robotics at Motorola, for a mobile phone assembly line. He had experienced a particularly bad day that week. We were under a lot of pressure to keep the production line running. Any malfunction that caused the line to stop meant the company was losing money, and whenever it happened the boys and girls in senior management heard all about it and got familiar with our names—and not in a good way. Anyway, my co-worker was sharing with his brother about the rough time he was having at work. His brother, who happened to be a doctor, made a joke about it, saying something like "What was so bad about your day? Did you lose a phone on the operating table?"

In other words, he implied that his brother's job didn't matter because he wasn't saving lives as doctors did. I could tell my friend was really affected by that comment. With a few words, the brother negatively affected my friend's life in a fairly profound way. It also did a serious injustice to the fact of how my friend's work was affecting other people's lives. As I said, our work was highly visible to senior management, and the reason is because our actions had an impact on the jobs of thousands of workers. Maybe we didn't save someone's life in a big way, but we helped in our own way to keep them employed and able to support their families.

It's true that sometimes we forget how what we do makes a difference and we need someone else to remind us of that.

Let me share a personal story that happened to me a while back, at a time when I was struggling with self-doubt and wondering what I was really doing. It happened when I was doing a gig with another singer-songwriter in old downtown Fort Worth, Texas at a place called the "Thirsty Armadillo."

To be honest, it wasn't even one of my better nights.

There was a booking agent in the audience, and I was a little nervous, and it wasn't one of my technically best performances. But--the other singer had been doing a lot of gritty, acoustic songs. So I chose to open with a more fun dance-y song I'd written. And then this young couple started to dance. After dancing for a while, the woman gave me a look that said everything: she was so happy dancing with her head nestled against her man's shoulder and grateful to me for playing the song. She just wanted him to hold her close, and that song was the opportunity she was waiting for. After seeing that, I threw out my planned setlist and played more dance songs instead so this couple could continue dancing in each other's arms.

Later when I wasn't on stage anymore, I was sitting at a table watching the next performer and the guy (of the couple) made a point of coming over to my table and giving me a tip. Some nights it's hard to get tips when you're on stage, and rarer still to get them when you're done. But with something as simple as a few right songs, I had *made this couple's evening*. And in return, *they touched mine*. That simple gesture made the hours of hard work and frequent rejection all worth it.

So you don't have to be a doctor saving lives on the operating to make a difference in someone's life.

I'm telling you my story to show you just one example of the many ways you can matter in someone's life without needing to have a special job or making a headlines-news-level accomplishment. Not everyone can be a billionaire like Sir Richard Branson or Elon Musk, or change the world as publicly and profoundly as Dr. Martin Luther King. These are great goals and by all means, shoot for the stars. But don't feel that if you don't accomplish such a bold achievement, then what you do doesn't matter. Changing the life of one human being in person affects them at a *deeper personal level* than a famous person who changes the world in general.

Getting back to the matrix, you want to be, or strive to

be, in the quadrant where you feel your work is enjoyable *and* also matters. Without both of these, it will be hard to sustain and be fulfilled. The strategy starts by figuring out where you are right now on the matrix. Be honest with yourself--you won't be able to make a change for the better if you don't. Also, you should consider this a journey. Where you feel like you fit in this matrix can and will change over time. It might even change to the good or bad in one day.

So sketch out the matrix and put a dot where you feel you are now. Once you determine where you are--and I'll assume it's not where you want to be exactly--you can start taking concrete steps to move that dot towards the quadrant of Enjoy and Matters. How do you make this happen? Well, your specific next steps will depend on which needs more improvement: Enjoy or Matters. But also you will use the tactic of this book, whose theme you have seen over and over:

- Identify your My One, the thing that matters most right now.
- Focus on your My One.

Summary:
Do more of what you enjoy.
Do more of what matters to you.
Change people's lives, personally, and one person at a time.

Get 1% Better Every Day

It's easy to get discouraged when you're knee-deep in a new project, starting a new career path or pursuing a dream goal. Once the initial euphoria wears off all you can see is all the hard work in front of you.

It's even worse if you start comparing where you are in your journey to people who are already successful or well into their journey. But your journey is just that: a road trip from where you are now to your desired destination. You need take it day by day and enjoy the scenery along the way. And even learn to appreciate the detours and gritty, non-glamorous stretches of the journey as opportunities to learn and grow.

The reality is that most of the time you won't make huge changes overnight. Sometimes you experience a breakthrough, but most of the time it's going to be slow, imperceptible improvement. And the imperceptible part is what makes it so frustrating.

What if you set a goal to get 1% better every day? You may be thinking that doesn't sound like a lot. It's going to take forever to reach your goal, right? How will you even notice that you got 1% better?

But let's do the math. If you get 1% better every day, that's *365% better in one year*. (366% better if it's leap year). How would you like to be over three and a half times better (faster, stronger, richer--fill in the blank) one year from now?

Now, that 1% per day is suddenly starting to sound too good to be true. Why don't we get amazingly better every year? The reason is because we get in ruts where we repeat the same efforts, in the same way, day after day, week after week, and sometimes year after year. Also, growth is not endlessly linear. When you start to reach world class levels of performance you will start to get diminishing returns. The difference between the gold medal and silver medal performance is milliseconds or a fraction of a percent. But on the plus side, hey, you're a world class performer! High five!

The reality is that you will fail to get better by 1% every single day. Maybe you will even get 1% worse some days. But if you stay the course, you will continue to get better and grow every year. What if you only got about 100% better every year? That sounds pretty amazing. What about only 50%? I'll take that too.

Another thing to remember is that there are so many ways you can get better as a person, that overall there is no limit to how much you can grow. If you peak at your physical goals, start a new skill from 0% and get 365% better at that.

Skills, talent, productivity, fitness, personal relationships, charity—the list goes on. So you don't, and maybe can't, get 3650% better, or even 1000% better at your core art, in ten years. But overall, when you include all the dimensions you can improve in your life, you *can* achieve these huge gains over time as a person.

Don't worry about the numbers. Just focus on accomplishing something each day whether it's learning a new micro-skill, pushing your performance a bit more or forming a new connection with someone. The numbers will take of themselves in the long run.

Summary:
To avoid getting overwhelmed, focus on getting 1% better every day.

Stop Lifting The Same Weights

If you going to start (and keep) getting more done with less work, you're going to need to do less. Very profound huh? But hear me out. The other day I was watching a video on Instagram from a "fitness mom." She was talking about how she regularly does an intense high impact leg routine followed by another intense cardio routine. She was proud of herself—and she should be. The problem was: with a regimen like that this woman should have looked like an amazingly buff, top-level fitness competitor. *She did not.* My intention is not to criticize her, but I wondered what was going on here?

Lets just politely remind ourselves that what's on the Internet does not equal reality. After watching some more videos I concluded that she was *"lifting the same weights."* She was probably working out regularly, but the routines she thought were intense—and probably felt really intense in the beginning—were more mediocre than intense. And she just kept doing the same level of workout over and over without pushing herself further.

In bodybuilding, if you want to keep growing or improving your muscles, you have change up your routine regularly. Quite simply: you have to "mix it up." It's quite common in the gym for someone to make some great muscle gains and then "plateau" (stay the same size), even though they are still putting in the work. One of the causes of this is that they keep lifting *the same amount of weight in the same way.* This results in your muscles getting used to the routine, and then they no longer have to work as hard. And as such they will not be stimulated to grow. In my experience, they might even lose some size. The result is you're mostly just burning calories and not getting the results you seek.

The general solution is to increase the weight you are using in an exercise, or increase the number of reps (repetitions of the exercise). It's a little more complicated than that (you can't just do a zillion reps with teeny, tiny weights), but you get the gist.

Another method is called the "muscle confusion principle." Bodybuilding experts don't agree on this (or anything else, actually) but experience in the gym says it works. The idea is to switch up your routine by throwing some totally new exercises at your muscles. This will "confuse" your muscles, wake them up out of their rut, and cause you to see some new positive results.

What in the world does any of this have to do with productivity and getting things done? Well, the muscle confusion principle works by *not doing the same thing over and over again* with diminishing results. By forcing your muscles to work at different angles, speeds or ranges your body kicks it up a notch to produce better results than you would have seen by doing the same routine. In other words, by doing Less work, More gains are realized. Less Is More strikes again by focusing on quality over quantity.

More importantly, we can apply this principle to other areas of life and getting things done. You want to look for ways to stop lifting the same weights, metaphorically. You're going to need to actively prune the practices you are doing that don't improve your important goals, and find new practices and tactics to throw into the mix. It doesn't matter if we're talking about fitness routines, self-improvement rituals, productivity tips or relationship-building.

Also, if you keep piling on more and more practices and rituals you are going to be back where you started: stressed out and getting diminishing results. Instead, replace a tired practice with a new one to get better results with the same or less amount of work.

I want you to approach this within the same mindset and framework though. You still should still focus on your core art and priorities, and you should work on them when your energy is high. But, *within that mindset*—think about how you can mix it up periodically.

To give other examples:

- Don't give up affirmations but freshen them up periodically.
- Can you find new tools to streamline your social media interactions?
- Can you spruce up your sticky note system? Do you need to start using one?
- Are you regularly reviewing your year goals to add new growth priorities, and not just working on the same ones in the same way?
- *And finally, are you always thinking about how to get 1% better every day, and not the same 1% you did yesterday?*

Summary:
Stop lifting the same weights, both metaphorically and literally (because fitness makes everything better).

Work-Life Balance

You have probably heard--or maybe even thought a lot about--work-life balance. It's a popular topic among self-help and motivational speakers, and I'm sure it will continue to be an important topic in our ever-more online and connected world. This is going to be a short chapter because this entire book is focused on improving your work-life situation by increasing your focus, reducing your stress, and improving the quality of both your work and non-work life.

We are certainly not the first generations in history to spend less time with our families because we are killing ourselves with long hours at work. I'm sure people who have worked in coal mines, on ships, military tours of duty and other highly committed and sometimes life-or-death jobs—well they would have little sympathy for us.

I think the difference is we now have more choices--maybe too many--and a never-ending barrage of media and cultural noise to make us doubt our choices and feel bad about ourselves and what we haven't accomplished yet.

The good news is by using Less Is More principles you can accomplish great things with your core art and still have a life—in other words, quality relationships with family and friends. In essence, the secret sauce is:

No matter how many things the world throws at you, now or in the future, you should focus on your current priority—your My One, as I keep saying. It doesn't matter how many things you're *not focusing on* because they don't matter right now.

Learn to embrace this strategy and work-life balance will take of itself. In fact, you may want to think of it as work-life abundance, because you will be able to accomplish—that is, actually finish or enjoy—more things, because you will free yourself from the limiting distractions and self-defeating practices.

You will have less stress in your life, because you start to realize and believe that you are making achievements, one focused step at a time. And you will also have less stress when you eliminate, minimize or delegate those exasperating and limiting urgent-but-not-important distractions.

Having It All, Just Not At Once

As I mentioned in the introduction, I don't want to give you the impression that Less Is More means you have to settle for less. I like More. I want More. And I want you to have More too: More of what really matters to you, and More time to focus and enjoy getting there.

I want to be a lot of things. I wanted to be a good entrepreneur AND a good husband and father. I never understood why I should have to choose. Sure, I almost certainly gave up becoming a rock star, dotcom millionaire because I refused to "go all in," ditching my day job, racking up huge debt and working breakneck 80 hour weeks. But what would I have given up in the process: killing my relationships and being an absentee father?

With the Less Is More strategy you don't have to give anything up. You just need to let it happen, and with the principles in this book, help make it happen one piece at a time when it's the right time.

Let's say at age 21 you dreamed of having your own fashion clothing line, but then life happened and you got a job, and got married, and had kids. But your dream never went away, except now you feel like you have no time and you missed your chance. And maybe you feel trapped and a little resentful. That is very understandable.

But let's look at it a different way. If you made your bucket list or dream list for your life what would it include? If you're like many people, it probably would include finding that special person to share your life with, and also include making a family. So from that perspective, you may be accomplishing those at just the right time. Don't let yourself be miserable and absent while your kids are growing up and then miserable again down the road when you think about what you missed. Instead, be present and enjoy what you have now, but realize you always have more chances to pursue your passions. Mindset is everything.

Examples of people getting their second (or third or tenth) chance can be found all around us and in the media. Start making that happen, one focus at a time, using Less Is More principles. In my own time, I have been a successful innovator at high tech companies, an entrepreneur, husband, father and part-time musician. I am still working on the last one and I may never be famous at it, but I am still achieving success on my own terms.

Let me offer you some other perspectives:

- I previously talked about Laura Vanderkam and 168 Hours. She is managing, quite nicely it seems, a multifaceted career as a speaker and author as well as a being a spouse, mother and homemaker (on her own terms).
- *Austin Kleon*[1] is a multi-disciplinary creator: a New York Times bestselling author of three illustrated books, speaker, and previously a web designer and ad copywriter. Kleon refuses to choose.
- *James Altucher*[2] was a hedge fund manager and re-invented himself as a variety of things: entrepreneur, bestselling author, venture capitalist, and podcaster. He has founded or co-founded more than 20 companies.
- *Tim Ferriss*[3] is an entrepreneur, author, podcaster and authority on a variety of life hacking pursuits. Ferriss clearly refuses to choose only one thing.

You may be thinking that these people are special cases, but if you were to look at their stories you would see there was no special advantage, luck or particularly fortunate circumstance that launched their successes. They put in the work, they stumbled and got back up, and they made their own luck where they could. They achieved success by, in some form, adopting a Less Is More strategy:

- Identify your My One, the thing that matters most right now.
- Focus on your My One.

By identifying and focusing on one thing at a time, over time, you can accomplish great things in multiple areas of your life. If you can focus and immerse yourself into one thing per month, you will have accomplished 12 amazing things by the end of the year. These could be in the same area: your core art and passion, or in multiple areas of your life to achieve that work-life balance. It sounds simple at a high level, but it can be incredibly hard in real life which I why I am giving you the tools in this book. I have done it, the people who stories I talked about have done it, and you can too.

Visualize Your Perfect Day

Visualization is a popular and powerful tool for self-improvement, performance improvement, and lifestyle change. The subject can fill an entire book, but the general idea is simple: picture yourself in your desired state-- achieving that high score in golf, living free of a habit you're trying to quit, or successfully working in a new career. And by doing so, you train your mind to believe that picture of success as reality and to start to "actualize" it (make it happen).

There are different techniques for visualization depending on the guru and your particular goals, but one version I really liked came from Mike Cernovich in his book *Gorilla Mindset*[1]. The technique is called "visualizing your perfect day," and as you can probably guess it involves picturing what your ideal day would look like sometime in the future when you've successfully made your desired self-improvement or lifestyle change. I think "perfect day" is a little unrealistic, because a perfect day might include winning the lottery while partying on a yacht with Jay Z and Beyonce, but you get the point hopefully.

This technique is valuable for a couple of reasons:

- It helps you define concrete and therefore actionable target goals instead of some general, vague dream (I want to be a rock star, I want to be rich).
- If you do it right, it really makes you think about what you *don't want to do*. And this can be a real

eye-opener and save you from wasting a lot of time.

For example my passion is music. A lot of people dream about being a rock star singing for screaming fans, living a glamorous lifestyle and people throwing money at them. But that is the TV sitcom version. Celebrities usually work hard to get where they are and work hard to stay there.

Similarly, office workers in cubes all over the planet dream about working for themselves and telling the boss to take their job and shove it. But any entrepreneur or small business owner can tell you about the 100 hour weeks and all the hassles that go along with a business. People don't always think about what it takes to get to their imagined dream life, or what it's really like if you're lucky enough to be successful.

Once you get your head down from the clouds, you can start to think about what success would really look and feel like for you. And you can consider and plan for the best lifestyle options that suit you and minimize the ones that don't. This exercise is effective even if you don't have lofty dreams and are just thinking about a job switch for example.

To perform this exercise you really want to visualize an average--but ideal--day, and walk through each hour or parts of the day. To get you started, Cernovich suggests some questions to ask yourself such as:

- Where do you wake up? What city? The country? A beach house?
- What do you do immediately when you get up? Coffee on the porch? Yoga?
- When and where do you work, on your job or

passions?

Be as thorough as you can with this visualization exercise and it may open your eyes to some things. Or at least it will help make sure you're not steering yourself into a daily lifestyle you won't really enjoy. And finally, I should say that any change or growth probably involves doing a lot of hard work to get there. That's to be expected, but it would be worse to "succeed" and still not enjoy what you're doing.

This is not intended to discourage you in any way. So for sure, dream big and shoot for the stars if you want. But use visualization to make sure it's the *right* star.

MORE Done Actions

1. Map out your New Matrix
2. Focus on getting 1% better every day.
3. Stop lifting the same weights.
4. Pursue it all--just not all at once.
5. Visualize your perfect day.

Closing Words

Any worthwhile change is going to take some effort and some time. However, I intentionally focused on simple systems and tactics so that they can be implemented and internalized quickly, so you don't get bogged down with a complicated new system.

Nor should you have to wait a long time to see and feel results, which would then cause you to get discouraged. I prefer, and embrace, principles and tactics that are effective *and* simple. I sincerely hope that after reading this book, this becomes your experience as well.

When you start to embrace the Less Is More mindset, you will start to feel a change—not just see it but *feel it*. Friction will start to remove itself with less conscious effort than before, because you will be subconsciously avoiding or managing it more effectively.

You will also start to feel some of your stress melt away because you will get more of your core art done, which is important to you, and therefore you will avoid the feelings of depression and resentment you had because you weren't getting them done. And—you will do this while still maintaining quality relationships with—and commitments to—other people and responsibilities, because you will focus on what is important and not what is, or pretends to be, urgent.

Finally, you will start to develop a creative spirit that is a little hard to put into words but is nevertheless *a real and awesome outcome* of internalizing Less Is More. You will be spending more time on creative work, and creativity promotes more spontaneous creativity. As an example, one day I was getting dressed and preparing to go to Starbucks to do some of the actual writing of this book. Suddenly I was spontaneously getting all these creative ideas for other projects and bits of copy (wording for written material). Of course I didn't allow myself to get defocused. I quickly captured some brief notes for later consumption so I wouldn't forget them, but then I proceeded to go to Starbucks to focus on my current My One priority.

My point is, on that day, it dawned on me that this kind of spontaneous creative flow was not happening very often in the past. Instead of enjoying a creative flow of ideas while I was taking a shower I was feeling rushed and stressed and distracted about the "urgent" work I had to get done—work that wasn't important to me in the long run. As I started learning, experimenting with, and curating the strategies and tactics that became the Less Is More mindset, I started to feel this real change in my schedule, reduced stress, an increase in getting things done that mattered, and—last but not least—an improvement in *how I felt about myself as a creative person*. And *you absolutely can* feel this as well. So without any further ado:

Go forth and do Less! Get More done!

Have More life,
Chris

A request...

Pretty please?*

Reviews are gold to authors! If you've enjoyed this book, would you consider rating it and reviewing it on amazon.com?

*Studies show, the physical attractiveness of the "please" *does,* in fact, make a difference.

Speaking Engagements

I would love to continue to be part of your lifestyle improvement journey. If you are interested in having me speak at your conference or company's event, you can get in touch with me at:

booking@chrisleespeaker.com

Let's do this!
Chris

Intro

1. "The obscure we see eventually. The completely obvious, it seems, takes longer."
Edward R. Murrow, https://allauthor.com/quotes/74064/
2. Mark Manson. Blog post "How To Be More Productive By Working Less". markmanson.net/how-to-be-more-productive, May 12, 2017.

Can you multitask?

1. The Myth Of Multitasking, Psychology Today, https://www.psychologytoday.com/us/blog/creativity-without-borders/201405/the-myth-multitasking

80/20

1. Richard Koch, The 80/20 Principle, The Secret Of Achieving More With Less, Crown Business, 2011.

Your Core Art

1. Jessica Hische, https://quotesondesign.com/jessica-hische/
2. Derek Sivers, https://sivers.org/compass
3. Derek Sivers, https://sivers.org/compass

21 Day Mastery

1. Ed Rush, The 21 Day Miracle, https://my21daymiracle.mykajabi.com/21daymiracle.
2. Ed Rush, blog post, March 10, 2016, https://edrush.com/how-i-wrote-a-288-page-book-in-7-daysand-how-you-can-too-even-if-you-failed-mrs-potters-3rd-grade-english-class/
3. Ed Rush, The 21 Day Miracle, https://my21daymiracle.mykajabi.com/21daymiracle.

Focus On Your My One

1. Gary Keller, The ONE Thing: The Surprisingly Simple Truth Behind Extraordinary Results, Bard Press, 2013.

* * *

Seriously, Just Focus

1. Timothy Ferriss, The 4-Hour Workweek, Vermilion, 2010.
2. Timothy Ferriss, The 4-Hour Body: An Uncommon Guide to Rapid Fat-Loss, Incredible Sex, and Becoming Superhuman, Harmony, 2010.
3. Timothy Ferriss, Tools of Titans: The Tactics, Routines, and Habits of Billionaires, Icons, and World-Class Performers, Houghton Mifflin Harcourt, 2016
4. Tim Ferriss, "Tim Ferriss: The Productivity Superpower You Didn't Know You Had", https://www.inc.com/video/tim-ferriss/the-productivity-superpower-you-didnt-know-you-had.html
5. Tim Ferriss, Productivity" Tricks for the Neurotic, Manic-Depressive, and Crazy (Like Me), https://tim.blog/2013/11/03/productivity-hacks/

What Would Easy Look Like?

1. Craig Bloem, Want to Be More Productive? Try This 1 Proven Tip From Tim Ferriss", https://www.inc.com/craig-bloem/this-1-tip-from-tim-ferriss-will-propel-your-startups-productivity.html

Important Versus Urgent

1. Quote Investigator, "What Is Important Is Seldom Urgent and What Is Urgent Is Seldom Important", https://quoteinvestigator.com/2014/05/09/urgent/

Defer Social Media

1. Freedom app, https://freedom.to
2. Cold Turkey Blocker, https://getcoldturkey.com

The Art Of the Graceful "No"

1. Greg McKeown, Essentialism: The Disciplined Pursuit of Less, Virgin Digital, 2019.

The Hemingway Method

1. Hemingway would stop his day's work in the middle of a sentence, one reference: Lifehacker, https://lifehacker.com/5278762/stop-writing-mid-sentence-to-ward-off-writers-block

Accountability Is Key

1. Association For Talent Development website, http://www.td.org

* * *

The 5 Second Rule

[1] Mel Robbins, The 5 Second Rule: Transform your Life, Work, and Confidence with Everyday Courage, Savio Republic, 2017.

[2] Mel Robbins, TEDx Talk, https://melrobbins.com/blog/the-5-second-rule/

168 Hours

[1] Laura Vanderkam, 168 Hours: You Have More Time Than You Think, Portfolio, 2010.

Go Analog

[1] Austin Kleon, Steal Like an Artist: 10 Things Nobody Told You About Being Creative, Workman Publishing, 2012.

The Minimum Viable Product

[1] Jason Fried and David Heinemeier Hansson, Rework, Currency, 2010.

Manage Energy, Not Time

[1] Jim Loehr and Tony Schwartz, The Power of Full Engagement: Managing Energy, Not Time, is the Key to High Performance and Personal Renewal, Free Press, 2003.

[2] Tony Schwartz and Catherine McCarthy, Manage Your Energy, Not Your Time, Harvard Business Review blog, October 2007, https://hbr.org/2007/10/manage-your-energy-not-your-time

Diagram: Energy

[1] Jayson DeMers, Blog post, Forbes, Apr 9, 2015, https://www.forbes.com/sites/jaysondemers/2015/04/09/is-sleep-deprivation-killing-your-chances-of-entrepreneurial-success/

Diagram

[1] Malcolm Gladwell, Outliers: The Story of Success, Back Bay Books, 2017.

Having It All, Just Not At Once

[1] Austin Kleon, https://austinkleon.com/about/

[2] James Altucher, https://jamesaltucher.com

[3] Tim Ferriss, blog, https://tim.blog/

Visualize Your Perfect Day

[1] Mike Cernovich, Gorilla Mindset, CreateSpace Independent Publishing Platform, 2015.

www.ingramcontent.com/pod-product-compliance
Lightning Source LLC
Chambersburg PA
CBHW060850170526
45158CB00001B/302